D1558726

Too Wise
to be Mistaken,
Too Good
to be Unkind

by Cathy Steere

With a foreword by Anne Marie Ezzo

Grace and Truth Books
Sand Springs, Oklahoma

Copyright © 1999
Grace and Truth Books
3406 Summit Boulevard
Sand Springs, Oklahoma 74063
(918) 245-1500
www.graceandtruthbooks.com

Cover design by Dennis Gundersen.
Back cover photo by Peter Walsh.

ISBN 1-930133-00-6

To every parent who is trying to find
his way through the maze, to the way of hope,
far away from the monster called autism—

and to every child imprisoned in its grip.

History Behind the Title

Samuel Medley was considered a great preacher and much-loved pastor during his years of ministry in the late 1700s. In addition, he penned nearly fifty hymns that were often written upon a significant event in the church or lives of church members or which pertained to a particular sermon he had prepared. The hymn with the phrase ending each verse, "Too wise to be mistaken, too good to be unkind," is believed to have been written upon the tragic death of a little child as a comfort to its mourning parents. Medley directs the parents to find their comfort in the wisdom and kindness of God.

—Mark McCormick

Contents

Foreword

You are about to embark on a journey with the Steere family as they travel along the mysterious road of autism. The very word *autism* draws fear and panic in the minds and hearts of parents who wonder about the unexplainable behaviors of their children. Where does a parent go to find some comfort and encouragement?

The majority of books written on this topic are either too clinical or convey a message of despair. This book is refreshingly different, offering hope to those who are faced with the challenges that accompany autism. The many factors that helped David and Cathy work through their emotions as they came to grips with the fact that their son Drew was having great difficulty in adjusting to the world around him will serve to strengthen the hearts of those who find themselves in a similar situation. Their continuing commitment to remain steadfast in consistently applying biblical principles creates the stability and predictability their entire family needs to face the challenges the Lord has placed before them.

Whether you are a parent dealing with an autistic child or a friend wanting to offer support and understanding, you will find in *Too Wise to Be Mistaken, Too Good to Be Unkind* that it was and continues to be David and Cathy's strong faith in a wise and good God that has been the sustaining presence in their lives. II Corinthians 1:3–4 reads, *"Blessed be the God and Father of our Lord Jesus Christ, the Father of mercies and God of all comfort, who comforts us in all our tribulation, that we may be able to comfort those who are in any trouble, with the comfort with which we ourselves are comforted by God."*

You will now become the beneficiaries of that comfort. As you read, be prepared to share in the joys and sorrows that brought Drew from "a prisoner in the silent world of autism" to the dear boy who now offers spontaneous acts of affection to his family. This testimony of God's grace will bring great hope to your heart.

To God be the glory,
Anne Marie Ezzo

7

Acknowledgments

I would like to thank Lorie Ann Grover who inspired me to write this book and gifted me along the way with encouragement, suggestions, and a listening ear.

Special thanks goes to Anne Marie Ezzo who kindly agreed to read through the very first rough draft of the manuscript and for offering her support of this work by writing the foreword.

Thanks, too, goes to Cyndi Ringoen for her help with some of the technical portions of the book as well as her contribution at the end. Most especially, thanks goes to Cyndi for her work with Drew, for she, without fail, has been there for us, offering direction and encouragement. We count her a treasure for her understanding of our son's unique needs.

I would like to thank our pastor, Tom Lyon, for his faithful preaching of God's Word over the past years and for his unrelenting reminder that all things are disciplined by theology.

I would like to thank my editor, Jill Jones, whose patience, input, and organization brought this project to completion, and to Janice Wells who found her for me. Janice, as well, was a constant source of encouragement during the daunting process of trying to find a publisher who would consider the importance and necessity of a work on this issue.

Thanks goes to Mr. Dennis Gundersen for his advice and support, and for helping with the distribution of this book.

My very special thanks goes to my dear husband; without him there simply would be no book.

Lastly, I would like to thank all of our friends and family who have been faithful to offer up prayers on our behalf to the sovereign God of the universe, Who holds all things in the palm of His hand.

1
A Foundation of Truth

The screaming in the night was intense. We had never heard him cry like this before. We sped to the nursery of our nine-week-old baby boy. My heart raced faster than my feet. Adrenaline pumped through my veins. My husband, David, and I pushed past each other. Who was making Drew scream so? What was terrorizing our son? An intruder? A monster? Not sure what we expected to find, David and I burst into the nursery together.

There was nothing unusual in the dark room. No monster that we could see. Drew's teddy bear grinned on the dresser. The mobile above the crib waited to be wound. All was exactly as it had been left just hours before when we had kissed our baby goodnight and tucked him in.

But when I looked down into the crib, I saw the reason he was so disturbed. Normally, we placed Drew on his tummy. He always preferred sleeping that way. Now here lay our tiny baby, feet kicking madly at the air, arms shadowboxing, lying face up—on his back. He was screaming his loudest and his cries were unmuffled by his sheets.

How could this possibly be? I wondered, scooping up my son to comfort him. I knew I was a novice at this mothering thing, but I was sure I had read somewhere that he still had several weeks before he should be able to roll from his tummy to his back.

David collected all the tousled receiving blankets strewn throughout the crib. His face reflected my own feelings of concern. Drew's screams were those of sheer terror. He was too young to experience such intense fear. The light from the hall shone on his tear-stained face. His head bobbed about as he tried to continue his flight for safety. His body was arched and stiff, and he pulled away from me. A terrible sense of fear gripped me. "C'mon, honey," I cooed, "Mommy's here.

Everything is okay."

Why couldn't I quiet my own baby? What was I doing wrong? My baby needed me. Why couldn't I give him comfort?

He didn't relax into my hug or lay his tiny head on my shoulder, but at last the intensity of his crying lessened. David and I worked together to wrap him up like a burrito in the receiving blankets. Nice and tight—that's how he liked it. We gently lowered him into the crib on his stomach. We put his head at the opposite end, away from the wet spot where his tears had soaked the crib sheet. After we left him, we could still hear him whimpering in the dark of his room. David held me in his arms in the hallway outside Drew's door. We listened. Drew finally settled down and fell asleep for the rest of the night. Gradually, our breathing calmed too. We had experienced his terror. How couldn't we? He belonged to us and we loved him.

David and I had diligently prepared for parenthood. We were as prepared to be parents as we thought we could possibly be—not just in the practical matters of caring for an infant, but also in our realization of the serious responsibility we had been given to train him. Throughout the pregnancy we had studied the different parenting styles and philosophies available to the new parent. We determined to utilize parenting materials which espoused these principles:

- The husband and wife relationship has first priority in the home.
- Parents are responsible for the moral development of the child.
- Routine is a benefit in the emotional, physical, social spheres and in the development of character.

We firmly believed that the most important issue in our new roles as parents was an understanding of the nature of God and the true nature of man. As to the nature of God, He is sovereign!

"For of him, and through him, and to him, are all things: to whom be the glory for ever. Amen" (Romans 11:36, KJV).

In his book, *The Sovereignty of God*, Arthur W. Pink answers the question, "What do we mean by this expression [the sovereignty of God]?":

> We mean the *supremacy* of God, the *kingship* of God, the *Godhood* of God.
>
> To say that God is sovereign is to declare that *God is God!*
>
> To say that God is sovereign is to declare that He is the Most High, "doing according to His will in the army of heaven and among the inhabitants of the earth, so that none can stay His hand" (Daniel 4:35).
>
> To say that God is sovereign is to declare that He is the Almighty, the possessor of all power in heaven and earth so that none can defeat His counsels, thwart His purpose, nor resist His will (Psalm 115:3).
>
> To say that God is sovereign is to declare that He is "the governor among the nations" (Psalm 22:28), setting up kingdoms, overthrowing empires, and determining the course of dynasties as pleases Him best.
>
> To say that God is sovereign is to declare that He is the "only potentate, the King of kings, and the Lord of lords" (I Timothy 6:15).
>
> Such is the God of the Bible.

To say that God is sovereign is to say that He exercises His will in the lives of each of His creatures—even in the life of our child. It is His sovereign will if He chooses to make our child deaf, dumb, blind, or handicapped in any way. He is the potter, we are but the clay.

How one views the nature of God impacts his perspective of everything that occurs in the world and to him personally. David and I recognized God's holiness, coupled with His power and control, in all events of life. This sovereignty is what makes Him God.

The other theological aspect we considered as new parents was the true nature of man. We knew the state of Drew's heart from the day he was born. Agreeing with the Bible, John Charles Ryle says it best in *The Duties of Parents*:

> Remember, children are born with a decided bias towards evil, and therefore if you let them choose for themselves they are certain to choose wrong. The mother cannot tell what her tender infant may grow up to be, tall or short, weak or strong, wise or foolish: he may be any of these things or not, it is all uncertain. But one thing the mother can say with certainty: he will have a corrupt and sinful heart. It is natural to us to do wrong. "Foolishness," says Solomon, "is bound in the heart of a child." . . . Our hearts are like the earth on which we tread; let it alone, and it is sure to bear weeds.

This quote asserts what is commonly known as the doctrine of Man's Total Depravity.

Our understanding of these two fundamental doctrines would be tested and tried in the years to come as it had never been before. That which would keep and sustain us through it all would be the wisdom and kindness of the one true God.

2
The Valuable Routine

Drew Alan Steere was a healthy-looking eight-pound baby. At his birth he filled his lungs with air and let the world know he was alive. From the first moment we laid eyes on him we could tell he resembled David's side of the family. He had dominant features and soft brown hair. His hands were big, like David's, and his head was perfectly round.

My pregnancy and labor were both normal and uneventful. Drew was monitored his first night in the hospital because of rapid respiration which, by the second day, was normalized. He was slightly jaundiced, but they let us take him home, for that, too, would quickly correct itself. He had a milkish film in his mouth, commonly known as thrush, we were told, that disappeared after several days of medication.

Everything seemed to be going great the first few days with Drew. We thought, "So what's the big deal with this parenting thing?" Then my milk came in.

No matter how hard I tried, Drew and I couldn't seem to get the hang of it. Our nursing sessions turned into frustrating crying events which ultimately led to screaming.

Drew cried, too.

For some reason, this perfectly normal human activity was the hardest thing to master. Drew would pull away and scream after several mad attempts to latch on. I felt like a huge failure as a mother. What was I doing wrong?

The only time David ever left me during our first week was to run to the store in an effort to find a bigger, better breast pump. I envisioned poor, shy David becoming a different person as he rushed into the store shoving people aside in a frantic attempt to purchase the best breast pump on the shelf. An auto mechanic by trade, he took his mission very seriously. But in spite of David's heroic efforts, Drew refused to cooperate with the team. We ended up bottle-feeding him and, with David's encouragement, I tried to cheer up. He reminded me that it wasn't whether I breast- or bottle-fed my baby that ultimately made me a good mother. Even so, I hadn't been prepared for this unexpected failure right off the bat.

Once the decision to bottle-feed was made, our lives quickly fell into a natural routine. We wakened Drew every three hours to feed him and then let him wake on his own in the night after the last feeding of the day. By three and a half weeks old, he was sleeping through the night. It wasn't long before our confidence began to grow. With every "well-baby" doctor's visit and every developmental milestone reached, we thought everything was fine with the world. Drew could track an object when moved slowly past his face and could hold his head up when on his tummy or being held. We couldn't have loved Drew more than we did. He seemed very content and never gave us cause for concern. Since all he really did at one month old was eat and sleep, the feeding routine made parenting seem like a breeze.

He grew fast and put on weight. He was robust and always ate well. The only thing I didn't care for was the constant burping up—at any time. At least for the first year of Drew's life, a cloth diaper slung over my shoulder was a perpetual fashion accessory to my wardrobe.

At four months old, Drew got his first sinus infection. The doctor prescribed an antibiotic which Drew detested. Trying to administer this drug was a test in creativity. If David was home, one of us held Drew's hands while the other tilted him back in his infant seat so that gravity could drizzle the bubble gum-flavored fluid down his screaming throat. When I was alone, which was the majority of the time, I had to somehow manage the entire operation. I remember thinking, *Why does he have to be so dramatic? The neighbors are going to think I'm trying to strangle him!*

Through what seemed to be super-human force and plenty of gurgling screams, Drew pulled through in the end and the infection cleared.

16

❖ ❖ ❖

One thing that happens when you have a baby is that suddenly you notice babies everywhere. Never before did you realize how many infants populated the earth. None, of course, are as cute or as smart as your own. The one constant, though, is that every baby acts as though his mother is the only person in the world. What baby doesn't crave his mother's attention?

After Drew was born I would watch babies at the grocery store as they tracked the every move of their mothers. The mother, oblivious, would continue with her task of determining the best buy on beef that day. When the mother would glance down at her worshiping infant, she would grin and begin a conversation in their own private language. Of course, the baby's face would light up as if someone had thrown a switch, and the secret language would continue to the point where both mother and child erupted with squeals of laughter. This seemingly universal language of love and delight between a baby and his mother was absent for Drew and me.

You can be sure I began to doubt whether I was showing Drew enough love and attention. Certainly, if I were, he would show just a little bit more need for me. He would seem happier when I talked to him and cuddled him. But not only did Drew refuse hugging and caressing, he acted as though I was personally assaulting him. With his screaming and pushing me away, I began to think he really didn't like me all that much. I knew I loved him, though. I tried to honor his repulsion of physical affection and chalked it up to the fact that he was a boy, thinking it was girls who preferred cuddling.

My greatest wish was that he would at least look at me. Drew almost constantly looked away whenever I tried to make eye contact with him. From the very beginning there was never any non-verbal interaction between us. I thought it was just his shy personality, but in periods of real doubt, I thought, *I am his mother. He could at least show me that he notices me once in a while.*

When Drew turned six months old, he discovered the ability for mobility. Enter a new phase in parenting. It was now time to implement the "teaching of boundaries." My four-legged blanket sleeper was pretty fast and took no time in discovering his vast environment. I watched him like a hawk whenever he got closer and closer to a forbidden object that was going to be used to teach him the difference between good and evil.

"No! Don't touch," I would say as I flicked the guilty hand.

David and I believed that all children, by nature, are fallen creatures and that disobedience is a natural consequence of a depraved heart. Our job was to train Drew's conscience. We knew we were unable to give him a new heart, but we knew we could and must develop his understanding of right and wrong. So it began.

"No! Don't touch." *Flick, flick.* "No! Don't touch." *Flick, flick.*

It was almost as if it didn't matter to him that he was in trouble. I started to think that God had given me the hardest-hearted child ever created. I kept up our training without relenting. I felt sure it would be just a matter of time before we would begin to see the fruit of our training. When corrected, he didn't cry and never appeared the least bit fazed.

We never felt we could trust him alone in a room, and we never wanted him to feel the satisfaction of disobedience. It was a tiresome job overseeing his journeys during his free time, which he was given throughout the day in between structured activities. We felt that the concept of learning boundaries was the most basic of concepts. Drew needed to learn it, not only for his own sake, but also for everyone's survival.

❖ ❖ ❖

Home life with Drew was stable but intense. From day one I ordered his schedule so precisely that I could account for every minute at the end of each day when David came home from work. Nothing was left to the chance that I'd have to resort to "response parenting." The schedule provided the order I needed to feel I was in control and functioning as a proactive parent, not an emotional, reactive one. Drew appeared to thrive under this structure.

I'd try to change activities approximately every twenty minutes or the moment just before I could tell he was getting bored. Here is a sample day:

> Mommy reading to Drew. Drew playing in the playpen with a few select toys. Mommy playing with Drew in the living room with block shapes. Drew looking at books in his crib. Mommy reading picture books to Drew. Drew in high chair with crayon and paper. Lunch. Nap. Drew playing in the playpen with different toys. Drew listening to music. Drew playing in living room with Mommy . . . .

I strove to provide the perfect balance between mother in charge and nurturing, attentive provider—the perfect atmosphere in which to train a child. I didn't really know what I was doing, so my confidence rested upon the scaffolding of a balanced routine. In that way, my day had goals and purpose, and Drew learned to take direction from me. It had an almost calming effect on him. Comparing this to the chaos he appeared to experience whenever we went out somewhere made us comment frequently to each other how remarkably sensitive our little boy was. Perhaps it was something he would outgrow.

3
Attempts at Socialization

The walls in our apartment were so thin we could actually hear our neighbor sneeze. Who knows what could be heard from us. At six months of age Drew was crawling like a professional. One day he was found standing in his playpen when he still wasn't able to sit up on his own. The banging began soon after that.

While in his playpen or crib, with the strength of a man, Drew would rock his prison so that it would actually leave the floor and then come back down with a loud BANG. Our neighbors who lived downstairs never complained to us, but they really didn't have an argument because they were prone to playing their music so loud we could feel our floor vibrate.

We decided that we would try to restrain his noisy habits to some degree, at least at those times he was in the playpen. We purchased four 10-pound weights at the thrift store and managed to attach them to each foot of the playpen. This helped protect the whole thing from flipping over, but Drew's strength seemed tempted by this new challenge. Not a bit discouraged, he forged on with the rocking—only this time I thought the floor might give way under the force of the added weight.

BANG, BANG, BANG, BANG, BANG.

As long as Drew was rocking, he was perfectly happy despite his imprisonment. The same was true in his crib.

Back at the time of Drew's birth someone had offered us their old crib, which we gratefully accepted. This old crib was extremely large and heavy, so we soon discovered that it worked just as well as the playpen in providing Drew's need for a motion "fix." We always knew when Drew had finally fallen asleep because the whole place was suddenly quiet as a tomb. We also were very aware whenever Drew woke up for the day. He would stay in his crib until I was ready to get him out in the morning. That meant that if he happened to wake at seven A.M. and I wasn't ready to get him out until eight, for a whole hour the building would shake with Drew's awakening.

Mealtimes were used as teaching events in our day. We introduced the sippy cup around Drew's first birthday. He had no clue what he was expected to do with that cup. I would pretend to drink out of it and make as many sounds of enjoyment as I could think of, but it had no effect on him. He wouldn't even watch me, and if he did spy his cup in my hand, he revealed no attachment to it and no desire to have it back.

Supposing this to be a device that his black heart had invented to oppose me, I made it a behavior issue. I refused to let him have his bottle, trusting that his thirst would become so unbearable he would have to take liquid from that sippy cup. After doing this a full day, however, I realized this was a potential health risk and resigned myself to giving him a bottle before bed so that he would get some fluid that day.

In spite of my efforts, he still made no move to use the cup and almost acted as if it were completely foreign to the whole concept of meal-taking. We persisted, though, considering the effects that giving in to his whims would have on his character development. Over a period of several months he did finally begin to show improvement. I was glad we had persisted.

When Drew was about one year old, he developed a physical inability to tolerate solid foods. The soft chunks in the number three baby foods were like huge chunks of steak to him. There was nothing more unappealing at mealtimes than serving Drew a small bite of "Chicken Dinner" and having him literally gag in our faces, unable to eat any of it. We had to stick to the number two baby food selections. We did manage to get cottage cheese and yogurt down him and oatmeal for breakfast.

When Drew was around fifteen months of age, mealtimes were still a chore because he still needed to be fed by hand. Gone were the days when David and I could just sit and relax and talk at the table over our dinner. Meals were work and hardly ever relaxing. David felt Drew needed to be made to take some of the mealtime responsibility for himself. I could tell that Drew didn't seem to "get it" when the time came to feed himself. His hands became like limp dishrags when we tried to position the spoon in his hand. The spoon soon became the focus instead of the food. We would take his hand and scoop up a bite and put it in his mouth. Letting go, we would think, "There, now this isn't so hard. Now go on and eat!"

But he would just pick up the spoon and stare at it as he watched the reflection of the light in it. It was as if nothing we had just done was registering with him. Playing the heartless teachers, we thought we would make him attempt eating on his own by not doing it for him. If he didn't eat on his own, he didn't eat that meal. He would then have to wait until the next meal and, being ravenous, would grab his spoon and dive in. At least, that was the plan. Since Drew had always been ambivalent toward food, our plan soon failed. He had never begged nor demanded food or drink. We simply had to remain consistent at encouraging him by putting his hand through the motions. It took a while, but like our efforts with the sippy cup, it finally paid off.

Drew had an undying need to learn about his surroundings through his mouth. We were constantly correcting him—"Not in your mouth!" —while removing the item from its slimy prison. It was a constant issue that got worse when his molars started to come in. The dear people who had lent us their crib would be shocked years later when they got it back. The crib's appearance would be slightly altered. When Drew wasn't rocking it across the floor in his room, he was madly chewing the rails on either end. There were teeth marks all around the top of the rails—some so deeply engraved we wondered at the strength of that little jaw. Not knowing any differently, we assumed this was the all-familiar "teething" stage that all babies go through. We couldn't have been more wrong.

❖ ❖ ❖

We put Drew in the church nursery when he was four months old. This was a difficult transition—for me. David tried to reassure me that it was a good thing for all of us. We would now be able to sit together and listen to the sermon without distraction, and Drew would learn to survive in someone else's care. It all sounded very simple, but it didn't change the fact that it was gut-wrenching to hand my baby over to someone else for an hour. Deep down I knew how sensitive he could be. It just seemed impossible for anyone else to know how to care for him.

That first Sunday he fared well enough, but over time things began to go downhill. Out of the handful of children in the nursery, Drew was the worst, crying and carrying on to an intense degree. I felt so apologetic whenever I left him. Instead of goodbye I mumbled, "I'm so sorry," to the nursery worker as I handed her my baby.

Drew would scream and cry the entire time, whether I was working in the nursery or not. I soon realized that it had nothing to do with me at all. I was a little hurt, but it obviously wasn't separation anxiety because he would scream even if I was there to do my best at comforting him. Once again I was met with a stiff little arched body that almost seemed to stiffen further under my comforting influence.

Slowly but surely my confidence as a mother was being shattered. What baby doesn't respond to the comfort of his own mother? Obviously, I was failing as a mother. It was now becoming embarrassingly clear to everyone observing me: my poor parenting skills could not be hidden any longer. The whole world was being made privy to it, it seemed. My own baby didn't even like me! Maybe all of those humanistic parenting magazines were right and my unborn baby had been able to detect my dislike for children. Had my inability to breast-feed only confirmed my psychological assault of my newborn? Maybe it was true that Drew never felt bonded to me. More than that, I had done this to him and his rejection of me was proof of it.

❖ ❖ ❖

Sundays became the worst day of the week and I soon began to dread going to church. I cried every Sunday afternoon when we got home.

"What am I doing wrong? Why does he freak out all of the time?" I blubbered at David one Sunday afternoon on the way home from church. "I just can't stand going every week only to have Drew scream the whole time. I never even hear the sermon. Why should I even bother going?" I finished with a dramatic blow of my nose.

David just gave a defeated sigh and offered, "I don't know, honey. I just don't know."

Putting Drew in the nursery his first year of life only increased my distraction from the worship service. The lack of participation in public worship and sitting under the preaching began to take a spiritual toll on me because in the middle of the sermon I inevitably heard his familiar faint scream coming up from the bowels of the church building. I'd get a sick feeling and think, "What now?" Racing out of the meeting room and flying down the stairs, I would hear my son's cries growing clearer and more intense. I would bound in to the familiar scene of frazzled nursery workers trying to bounce and comfort a screaming, stiff Drew. Nobody could give an explanation for what caused the uproar. I would apologize profusely to the nursery workers for my son's behavior and whisk him out of the dreadful room. This was the only cure to calm him. The only other place to go with him was up to a little room partitioned off from the large meeting room and reserved for nursing mothers.

By the time Drew was thirteen months old we quit trying to put him in the nursery. We felt like failures. So many well-intentioned people advised us not to give in to him. "He is obviously rebelling against your authority. My son was the same way—he hated the nursery, too. Don't let him win," they would say. The last thing David and I wanted to do was give in to Drew's demands. The problem was, it was hard to see his tears and shrieks as "demands." They looked more like "terror" to us.

24

❖ ❖ ❖

Since the nursery experience at church was no longer an option for us, and church was pretty much the only place we ever went together, we had only one choice before us: I needed to train Drew to sit upstairs with us in the service.

The children at our church were graduated from the nursery at the age of two to begin sitting with their parents in the worship service. Drew was still so young, but we really could not see any other choice, except to not go at all, an option I would suggest to David after church every Sunday in an outburst of emotion. But David would wisely say that we were just going through a season. It would not always be like this and we needed to remain faithful in our attendance.

So I began our training sessions at home on a daily basis. With Drew on my lap and a small pile of books by my side on the couch, I turned on the timer for five minutes. We were going to role play sitting at church. Drew was allowed a match box car to hold.

In our first session Drew, not liking this close proximity to me, tried to squirm away. I quickly corrected him, "Sit still." Handing him a book, I turned the pages slowly, which worked until the timer finally went off. I flipped out and praised Drew for sitting so nicely.

"What a good job sitting like a big boy—so quiet with no fussing!" I said, while setting him free right away. Drew showed no sign of pleasure that he had pleased me and quickly began lining up his cars on the piano.

The next day we attempted a reenactment. Drew's initial squirms were met with the same correction. "Sit still," I whispered in his ear. Although he didn't cry, he stopped moving and sat still. He kept himself busy with the Matchbox car, spinning its wheels over and over again. The timer, set again for five minutes, seemed to me to be stuck in time. Drew, getting bored with this setup, squirmed again and met the same consequence as before. He fussed at this and, to show his opinion on the matter, dropped his car on the floor. "No," I whispered in his ear, picking up the car and handing it back to him. He dropped it again. "No," again, only this time flicking his offending hand. Drew tried it again, showing no remorse. "No." *Flick, flick* on the hand. This now made Drew mad and he gave me one of his intense cries of frustration. My eyes welled up with tears. *What am I doing to this poor little guy?* I thought.

I continued our training sessions for lack of any other options. If Drew couldn't learn to sit for a short period, we would certainly become imprisoned ourselves, unable to even attend church.

This training process continued on a daily basis with flicks becoming less and less frequent and the length of sitting time growing longer and longer. He was learning. I would always try to end our sitting sessions with loads of praise, even if he had sat nicely only for the last few minutes. By eighteen months old, Drew was sitting through most of the services at church. If he seemed unusually restless, we would take him out of the service and down to one of the empty classrooms to play until the service was over. We never disciplined Drew at church or took him out for bad behavior. All of our training was done at home. Church was just the moment of truth—the ultimate test of how well we had done our job at home.

One of the things that dismayed me about Drew was that he hated it when I sang to him. Now I know that I'm not the world's greatest singer, but I also know that I'm not the worst either. All of the baby books say to sing to your baby—"They love it!" Well, not only did my baby not love it, he despised it. Once again I was met with that horrid cry and struggle to flee whenever I tried to sing to him. It didn't matter what song it was, Drew hated it. He would shriek and pull away even if I sang really softly or from another room. Needless to say, this didn't encourage my confidence—until we noticed that he responded the same way at church when the congregation began singing a hymn. David would rush out of the meeting room, trying to muffle Drew's screams on the way out so as not to disturb anyone with the wails of our child. When the people would finish singing, David would return with a now-quiet child, back to the books and Matchbox car.

The only thing we could do was try to not let Drew become a burden to anyone at church. This felt like a full-time job, one that left us pretty exhausted by Sunday evenings. But we weren't going to give up on going to church. We knew that we couldn't.

Our troubles with the nursery and church became life-consuming. It was the only place we ever really went. Drew always seemed to do fine while at home on his predictable routine, but if we went somewhere, just stopping at a stop sign would send him screaming in his little carseat. He would never fall asleep in the car and he got so worked up whenever we came to a complete stop. To remedy this, David would try to slide through some stop signs or take a different route. Anything to avoid the terrible screaming! It was so much easier on all of us to just stay home and stick to our schedule, but we concentrated our efforts on at least getting to church every week.

Many people become your "personal baby counselors" when you give birth for the first time. These self-made experts love to inform you, the ignorant caregiver, of all of the tips that should make your life with your new little baby easier. I don't know how many people who happened to see me with my crying baby in public or at church would soothingly counsel me that with experience comes the ability to distinguish your baby's cries. Over time, they said, I was going to become accustomed to knowing, by simply listening, if my baby was hungry, or tired, or sick, or just wanted a little loving. Despite all of my efforts at listening intently to determine the need of the moment, however, I always heard only one cry. It was a cry that would make me sweat and my heart beat faster. This was a cry of pure anxiety. This was a cry of sheer terror. This cry was always the same. Once it started, nothing would make it stop.

In people's attempts to fix my obvious mothering difficulties, they would offer me kind advice. One mother from church suggested I take Drew to the play pit at the mall. This effort would help the oversensitive child become more accustomed to being around other children. After this exposure, he might be able to tolerate the nursery situation better. More socialization—that's all he needed.

Though not believing in the over-emphasized need for socialization merely by exposing children to other small people like themselves, I considered it this time because I had nothing else to try to help Drew cope in this realm. Perhaps I had cloistered him too much and it was because of this that he was having such a difficult time in the church nursery. I made arrangements with a friend of mine that had a little girl Drew's age to meet us at the mall.

I was nervous, as I was anytime I took Drew somewhere. I never knew what might set him off. After parking the car, I buckled Drew into his stroller and we entered the mall to find my friend. We met up with her and her daughter and then we were off to find the play pit. All went well as long as the stroller I was pushing him in kept moving. He seemed intrigued with the bustling pit as we approached it. Children were running around a giant, soft train. Some were climbing to the very top of the steam engine and others were just running around the circular play area. A bench encompassed the entire pit for mothers to sit on and watch their young at play.

My friend and I approached the entrance to the play pit and read the sign to parents before entering the circle. We were to leave strollers at the entrance; they were not allowed in the play area. Nervously, I removed Drew from the stroller and we descended the stairs to the moving crowd of laughing children.

"Run!" I encouraged Drew.

He acted like he didn't know what was expected of him, even with the example of all the children scurrying past him. His face was serious as usual and he wore a look of lostness as he stood by my side. His concern for the stroller we had left at the entrance was greater than his

28

interest in the colorful train which stood before him. He didn't appear afraid, which I was quickly thankful for, but neither did he seem excited to be there as you would expect a child to be.

My friend and I found an empty spot on part of the bench to sit and talk and watch our children socialize. My friend's little girl was different from Drew in every way I could think of. She chattered and interacted—not just with her mother, but with me too. She laughed and played and ran, just like the other children. She would stop now and then to play a peekaboo game with her mother from behind the giant train. My friend would stop our conversation to laugh at her animated daughter and begin again when the little girl became interested in a game some other children were playing.

Where was my Drew? My eyes scanned the arena, checking each child coming at top speed around the turn. *Is he climbing perhaps? Or hiding around the train waiting for me to notice him so that we could engage in a game of peekaboo?*

After a moment, I spotted my little boy. He was separate from the crowd of children, kneeling on the top stair at the entrance to the pit. It was as if he knew instinctively that the pit was his boundary. Nothing the play pit had to offer was of interest to him. His sole focus was on the row of stroller wheels parked at the pit's entrance. He was trying so hard to reach the wheels; he had to lie on his tummy with his feet hanging into the pit boundary to just run his fingers over those blessed wheels . . .

As time passed and children came and went, my friend and I decided to call it a day. The objective in visiting this play pit had been to help Drew get used to the noise and play of children and to desensitize him to cope with life at church. But all that I accomplished that day was frustrating Drew by keeping him from what he wanted more than anything else: the wheels of a stroller.

There had never been a time in Drew's life so far that he hadn't shown a love for wheels. I thought this obsession made him "all boy." At fifteen months old his love for wheels was peaking. Drew would happily sit for an hour just watching cars come and go in a parking lot. He would get an eerie, transfixed look in his eyes tracking a car's every move. If we weren't fast enough, he would have his hands all over the exterior of a parked car, stroking its every line and running his fingers over the tires. I'm surprised we never set off any car alarms.

His reward for sitting nicely in church was to run and stand on the front steps of the church building where he would have the best spot to watch the parade of cars leaving the parking lot.

One night in particular Drew's obsession with cars and wheels caused me to experience a sinking feeling in the pit of my stomach.

It was a rather cold and rainy winter day here in the Pacific Northwest. The wind was blowing and the rain was coming down fast and at a slant. After the evening service I allowed Drew to escape to his post, not knowing how bad the weather was. After a short time I went to peek on Drew. I opened the front doors of the warm, crowded church to what looked, at first glance, like a typhoon. There stood Drew—frozen like a statue on the dark steps, his coat and hat dripping wet. He was all alone. His serious face showed no signs of disturbance at the elements whirling about him.

As cars drove out before him, Drew seemed mesmerized by each spinning wheel that passed by. The water splashed around each wheel as it turned. The family in the car would wave their biggest wave to Drew, seeing him standing there faithfully in his spot on the step. Drew waved, but not at the people. He waved at the beloved wheels going to their home for the night. Drew didn't ever seem to notice people.

Drew's obsession with cars and wheels was evident in his play. Cars, trucks, and trains—anything that rolled—was acceptable. His cars would never drive anywhere in particular, and he would never provide sound effects for them. I saw, after countless hours of watching him, that it satisfied him to just watch them roll back and forth at eye level. If he wasn't rolling them back and forth, he was lining them up in a perfect line. If, for some reason, they didn't all fit or line up just the way he felt they should, he would break down in that fierce cry—the only cry Drew ever had.

In an attempt to help Drew become a more social creature, David and I tried a new idea. From the time Drew was just a month old, I had made the reading of picture books a major part of his day. My original intention in these reading sessions was to cultivate Drew's attention to an activity and to teach focusing skills, self-control, and patience. Patience he would learn because it was I who said when we were going to read and when we were going to stop reading.

Our sessions began at five minutes several times a day and increased to twenty minutes. Eventually we increased them to one hour a couple of times a day. As I watched the slow improvement in Drew's ability to focus and get self-control, I knew I would never regret doing this for him.

With all of this reading of books, a weekly trip to the public library became as routine as stopping by the gas station to fill up the car. We were becoming acquainted with several of the librarians who checked our books out every week. Seeing our preschool-aged child, they frequently reminded us of the summer reading program.

"You really should bring him—the kids just love it," we heard.

David and I thought it just might be a good way to expose Drew, in a more controlled setting, to other children in a group situation.

The following Monday morning David, Drew, and I arrived at the library for reading circle. Little carpet squares set on the floor in a semicircle faced a chair at the front of the room. We all found our places on carpet squares, with Drew sitting on my lap and me sitting cross-legged. The room quickly filled up with other children and parents.

Suddenly, a door swung open up near the chair. The librarian in charge of story time reminded me of an old school marm. Her flat shoes

31

softly took her to the chair where she landed with a sigh and set a few select books on the floor next to a bag.

We hadn't even begun the first story and I could sense Drew's boredom. He tried to shove his hips off my lap. I held him down and began to get nervous. Why did we have to sit in the front row?

The librarian slowly worked through the first book, taking at least ten seconds to display the open picture to the group before turning the page. By this point I was starting to have to physically restrain Drew. He was lost in this group situation, not even realizing he was being read to. I looked around at all of the other children, sitting in rapt attention anticipating the next picture. They all seemed to not only understand what they were there for, but appeared to be enjoying it. Why did Drew have to be so difficult? Why did he have to oppose us at every turn? I couldn't leave—there was a sea of people on carpet squares blocking us from the door!

Finally, after finishing two books, our leader suggested we all stand up and stretch. I was glad for the little break, but Drew acted as though he thought we were done and it was time to go. While everyone else stretched, David helped me clutch Drew and return to our spots on the floor. The chaos in the room was beginning to make Drew anxious. After a time, everyone was back in place and ready for more.

Rather than reading another book, the librarian slyly pulled a green puppet out of the bag near her chair. My first thought was, *Uh oh, Drew is going to freak out for sure.*

It was explained to us that this little green dragon was Puff, her friend. He would soon be our friend as well.

David gave me a doubtful glance.

All the children began to talk excitedly the moment the fuzzy green visitor made his entrance. The woman with the puppet on her hand lumbered down off her chair to her knees, visiting each child with a greeting from Puff.

"Would you like to pet Puff?" she asked.

Of course, all of the children could barely contain themselves as they waited until Puff got to them. All of the children except one, that is. Drew took one look at the fuzzy face closing in on him and without warning gave Puff a good, swift kick in the face. From the look on Puff's friend's face, we could see that this was probably the first assault on Puff in the history of his visits to story circle.

We never returned for the summer reading program . . . and nobody ever asked us why.

4
From His Head to His Toes, a Perfect Creation

Despite Drew's odd ways, we couldn't have loved him more. I never dreamed so much love could come from me for a child, of all things. He was my world, my firstborn son, my dear sweet boy. I had experienced pregnancy and childbirth and caring for a newborn for the first time in my life. I had been with Drew from his beginning, and it would never be the same with another. All of the newness that surrounded his existence was what made him so special to me.

Lying next to David one night in bed, I could tell from his breathing that he was still awake. I told him how I loved him and that my life couldn't be any sweeter than it was with him next to me and our dear, perfect son sleeping soundly in the next room. Why had God seen fit to be so good to us in this life? We both knew full well how very undeserving we were and that it was simply the Lord's goodness and nothing else.

David held me close and prayed, thanking God for the many blessings He had given us together . . . and mostly for Drew.

After David fell asleep, I lay awake and wrote a song about my Drew.

> The news came one day, in the month of December.
> My feelings were not very clear,
> A little bit happy, a little bit frightened:
> I tried to decide through my tears.
>
> My feelings were shared by my husband beside me,
> Whose love and devotion were mine.
> It was hard to imagine that soon things were changing.
> It was now just a matter of time.
>
> We had nine, nine, nine months to go,
> A nursery to make, and a tummy to show.
> A baby was coming to our house to stay;

The plans were in motion as the clock ticked away.

The summer seemed hot and not all that friendly
To the frame of a mother-to-be.
My shoes wouldn't fit, and I felt oh-so-heavy.
The waiting now seemed drudgery.

The day finally came that had long been awaited,
And I looked to my husband with fear.
He took both my hands and said, "Try not to worry;
You know that I'll always be here."

It was time, time, time for the baby,
To meet him, to hold him, to give him his name.
A baby was coming to our house to stay,
We would be parents by the end of the day.

He was mine, mine, my little baby,
My eyes drank in all of his beauty.
From his head to his toes, a perfect creation.
I couldn't believe he was mine. I couldn't believe he was mine.
I'm so happy because he is mine.

One of the developmental stages David and I could hardly wait for was talking. We longed to engage in some kind of dialogue, however primitive, with our little human that lived with us. But this seemed to be taking a long time in coming. The main form of communication from Drew was his freak-out cry. Even that wasn't to demand anything from us—food, drink, or even a toy. Nor was it even to command our attention or remove him from his crib. He never called for me. How I longed to at least hear "Mama" in his cries. His cry was almost always associated with intense frustration or fear.

When people would say to us, "Just be patient. You should be happy.

Once they start talking, you just want them to quit!" I couldn't imagine it. It's only natural to desire to communicate with someone you love. How else can you really know them? People communicate with their pets and get more non-verbal results than we were getting with our son.

"Just be patient," I would hear. "Boys are always slower when it comes to talking."

Maybe the wait wouldn't have seemed so long if he had at least babbled and made some obvious sign that he was trying to talk to us.

Drew was always silent . . . except when he was crying.

Drew got sick several times his first two years of life. Being sick meant throwing up and having a fever and runny nose. Each time it happened, I hated it. It was almost as if I was the target whenever he had the urge to heave. The sickness was always sure to hang on for a full fourteen days, long enough to require antibiotics and missing church for two weeks in a row. My face would flush with guilt as I faced all of the nursing mothers at church, for everyone knows that babies who are nursed with that pure, magical breast milk virtually never get sick. This was just another slam against me—incompetent mother that I was.

There was one treasure hidden amidst the many changes of clothes and sheets and floor washings that sickness brought to our home. For the two weeks that we endured Drew's sickness, he, although obviously suffering, was uncharacteristically relaxed, even calm. He would just lie in my arms and look at my face with the most pitiful look of near death. I hate to admit it, but I took advantage of him. David would come home from work and I would greet him with a big smile. "Drew's sick!" I would cuddle Drew in my arms and sing softly to his face. He would show no sign of fright or flight and would allow me to actually caress his head and face. I, of course, was in heaven.

Despite his usual lack of eye contact and absence of language, Drew had perfect hearing. We had wondered at one point if there might be something wrong with his hearing because of his inattentiveness to us. However, because of his sensitivity to singing, we knew he could hear just fine. In fact, watching Drew play on the floor of the living room with his cars, I was often amazed at his heightened sensitivity to the sound of the refrigerator kicking on in the kitchen. He would jump, kicking his perfectly ordered line of cars. With a panic-stricken face, he would look in the direction of the kitchen.

He would become easily startled if I unexpectedly stood up from my chair too quickly. He would jump and begin to cry as if a bomb had just gone off in the room. My efforts to soothe him never worked and usually just made him cry more intensely.

I was often amazed at his interest in and apparent concern over the order of the room. If a pillow was out of place on the couch, he would cry and scamper to right it. My first thought was, *My, you are going to make some woman very happy in the future.* But this thought quickly turned into, *What is with you? It's just a pillow!*

I thought that maybe my routine at home was turning this poor boy into an obsessive, compulsive nut case. Someone even alluded to the fact that I must be doing this to him because, well, "Just look at how neat your house is!"

That's all I needed to boost my already-crumbled confidence in my own childrearing. Who else was there to blame? He was only with me all of the time. No one but me . . .

Doctor visits were never an enjoyable experience for anyone involved. Each "well-baby" visit just got worse the older Drew got. I began to despise the nurses because they usually made matters worse.

"Ohhh," said one, "is that an engineer hat? Do you like trains? Why don't you take all of your clothes off and sit up here for me. That's right. C'mon now."

This, all said with a shrill, high, penetrating voice—directed right in Drew's face.

He, needless to say, acted terrified in their very presence. I didn't think a person became a pediatric nurse unless she loved children and felt she had a special way with them, but these nurses appeared offended over Drew's resistance to their kindness and attention. His piercing scream and efforts to flee were met with an obvious "Humph" directed at me. Their glares implied that it was my mothering that interfered with their inability to make friends with him.

Matters did not improve with the entrance of the doctor. His touching and probing made Drew tighten up all the more. In fact, he did his best screaming for the doctor. I always felt as though I had betrayed my little boy when I reached for him after he had been given a shot. It usually took two adults to hold him down for those and, despite the struggle, Drew became stronger rather than weaker. With a red, blotchy face and tears dripping all over his half-naked body, he acted as if we were administering more than a routine vaccination. "Certainly they must be out to kill me," said his sweaty, resistant arms and legs.

I said to myself, *I wish she would just shut up*, as the nurse jabbered at Drew, putting a Mickey Mouse Band-aid over the fresh puncture in his thigh. Her voice and her persistence were more irritating than Drew's vocalizations.

Although these trips to the doctor were stressful, the doctor himself was very kind. He always took a lot of time with us and patiently listened to our problems or concerns.

On Drew's eighteen-month "well-baby" check up, I decided to share some concerns I had over Drew's oversensitivity to life. I dramatized our son's behavior to help paint an accurate picture for the doctor. As I spoke, his face slowly darkened with concern.

"What is it?" I asked him abruptly.

"Well," he chose his words carefully, "sometimes autistic children act the way you've described."

I responded with a confident laugh. "No way, he's not autistic!"

The word *autism* conjured up a bleak vision in my mind of a retarded, rocking child, unreachable and completely unaware of his surroundings. I even envisioned him drooling and banging his head against the wall. This was not my Drew.

My son certainly noticed people. He cried at them, didn't he?

Backing down, the doctor asked us to just keep him informed of Drew's progress and to let him know how his language was coming along.

I left the doctor's office that day completely satisfied that all was well with our little boy. I mean, every baby develops at his own rate, and you can't put a lot of stock in all of those developmental charts anyway. At least that's what I had been told.

5
Rite of Passage

David had spent a great deal of time and sweat fixing up our little apartment. One of his endeavors included installing a ceiling fan in our tiny kitchen. What a help this was to me! I despised the windowless closet and stale air and had convinced David that a fan was all I needed to become a really good cook—I mean, "A fan would make me want to be in the kitchen all of the time, cooking up fantastic meals!"

David bought this line and soon the project was completed. A white fan now spun above me in the kitchen. Now it was my turn to follow through with my promise. Stirring a big pot of spaghetti sauce one evening, I glanced down at my darling child who had crawled over to be near me as I slaved over the stove. Thinking sweet thoughts about how my son loved my very presence and would rather be here with me in the kitchen than anywhere else, a feeling of disgust replaced my happy thoughts. Soon I discovered I was not the focus of his attention, for, sitting there in the doorway of the kitchen, Drew had become mesmerized by the spinning fan above. Motionless, he was content to just watch it twirl. I, of course, was a little hurt. It wasn't me at all that he wanted to be near. I really don't think he even noticed me standing there.

When Drew was a little over two years old, he developed some very startling behavior. We would be coming home from church or the store, and without any warning, Drew would begin thrashing and screaming in his carseat behind me.

"What's the matter with him?" I gasped, turning around.

"Who knows," moaned David as he swerved back into his lane after being startled by the blast from the backseat.

Over time it became apparent to us that it was a particular intersection where we always made a left turn that set him off. All of a sudden, for no reason apparent to us, Drew would make it very clear that he thought we were turning the wrong way.

Part of me pitied him because his disturbance over the matter was so intense and irrational. It even seemed to increase with intensity over time. My only thought, however, was that in spite of whatever was triggering this fear reaction in him, he just could not be allowed to become so out of control. The only thing I could think to do at the moment was to turn around and, with my disapproving tone and a quick flick to his mouth, tell him, "No fussy. You need to get self-control."

My words seemed to just float out his window, but the flick to the lips startled him. When applied consistently over a few weeks' time, this behavior slowly subsided.

Drew was difficult to live with in the sense that he made you feel that anything—without warning—could set him off into an anxiety attack. One of the things that always bothered him was the vacuum cleaner. His response was so intense I was reluctant to vacuum. One time I even let a whole month go by without vacuuming. Even though I preferred my house to be clean, I preferred more to not put Drew through such agony. The terrific explosion that would emit from such a little person was unbelievable to witness. The terror in his eyes and desperation to flee really left me with no other choice.

I even tried closing him in his room to help muffle the sound of my cleaning. But when I shut off the beastly machine, Drew's wails could be heard piercing through the walls. Holding him and trying to soothe him with soft words after vacuuming each room did absolutely no good. What was I to do?

My plan of action eventually came down to cleaning at top speed. Drew still freaked out, but I felt I could at least shorten the duration of the torture for us both.

Taking a bath—a natural, everyday experience in any home—was another horror we inflicted on Drew. Some mothers I talked to only raved about how their children loved their bath.

"She cries when I take her out," one mother told me.

Picturing this in my mind, I saw how completely opposite it was to reality in our home. Drew didn't whine or cry because a bath was interrupting his play, he screamed and thrashed because the water was touching his body. He couldn't stand the way it trickled down his arms and back when we washed him off.

The worst of it came when we washed his hair. I was sure our neighbors would call the police because of the way Drew's screams were enhanced by the bathroom's abundant porcelain. No talking or soothing made a drop of difference. As with the vacuuming, our only option, besides never bathing him, was to do it only when necessary and as quickly as possible.

David and I settled on a once-a-week bath scheduled for Saturday nights. We had to work together to accomplish the task. Drew didn't improve over time and reacted the same way each time we washed his hair. Judging from the intensity of his fight, one would think we were shooting him in the head with rubberbands instead of simply washing his hair.

Along with bathtime came the eventual need to trim toenails and fingernails. His reaction to this activity was as strong as it would be if we were trying to amputate entire limbs.

"Why does he have to be so dramatic? The neighbors are going to think we're attacking him!" I cried, getting a better hold on Drew's feet so David could clip.

David had no answer and just continued with the "assault."

One neighbor actually did stop me in the hall one day and commented in an accusatory tone, "Man! What were ya doing to him the other night? It sounded like you were trying to kill him!"

"Yes, well," I blushed, looking down. "He is just extremely sensitive," I finally managed.

"Hmph" came her stiff reply before looking me up and down and closing the door of her apartment behind her.

My answer sounded so feeble before her accusation. But it was true! Drew *was* sensitive, very sensitive, about everything in life. It was almost as if he didn't even belong on this planet . . . everything about our world was so offensive to him.

Not long after Drew's second birthday David and I felt it was time for Drew to receive his first haircut. I hated to part with those beautiful golden curls that encircled his head like a misappropriated halo. Drew was such a beautiful child, even though his expression seemed permanently fixed in an anxious frown. His skin was creamy and velvety soft, and his eyes, the color of sapphires, were lined with a double row of dark lashes. His lips were full and perfectly shaped. Though he rarely smiled, he gave the appearance of maturity. But the day finally came to rid him of his baby curls.

We set him in his high chair and gave him a crayon and paper to help him sit through the styling process. I began snipping away with the scissors and soon the job was completed. His new look gave him a much older air. Drew never colored with the crayons we provided for him, but the routine rolling of them across his paper helped keep him somewhat busy until I was finished. His style soon grew out and this time a professional cut was in order.

David had always had Paul of Paul's Barber Shop cut his hair. I would always tag along and sit there to wait for him. It was an activity that usually interrupted one of our other errands. Of course, I felt out of place with all of the other men in the room. The TV was always on and it amused me to see so many people in one room fixated on a golf game. If the men weren't watching TV, it was the sports section of the newspaper that held their attention. It was always tomb-quiet except for the buzz of the clippers—no chatter like there was at the beauty salon I frequented.

We all arrived one afternoon to get haircuts for David and Drew. It was hot and the sun blazed through the window. The TV was on as usual and the collective stiffness of the patrons worsened as I entered the room. I felt I was intruding on some sort of private male experience. I sat there, nevertheless, because my little boy was making the life-changing transition into manhood that day: a haircut from the barber. I felt I had a personal right to witness this rite of passage.

Drew hopped up next to me on the bench to wait for Daddy to get done. He held his Matchbox car and rolled it between us on the bench, having no clue of the magnitude of his upcoming experience.

When David was done getting sheared, it was Drew's turn. Drew acted a little bewildered when David swung him up on the booster chair that had been placed on the spinning throne. The scene was picture-perfect until the clippers buzzed near Drew's head.

"AAAAAHHHHHHHHHHH," screamed Drew.

Wincing, some of the older patrons adjusted their hearing aids. I started to feel very hot. The sun felt like fire on my face.

I should have known this wasn't going to be an easy process. Nothing ever is with Drew, I thought to myself.

The look on Paul's face was that of grave concern and seemed to be asking, "What should I do?"

"Just do it," I exclaimed emphatically, getting a grip on an arm and a leg, David taking the other side. We held Drew captive during the whole torturous, buzzing process. Drew, thrashing and screaming as if being unduly harmed, was the center of attention of the entire shop. We received looks of "What on earth . . . ?" I thought that surely this wasn't the first time a child had gone berserk at the barber shop. But according to the looks on all their faces, no child ever had in the history of barber shops.

Piling into the car, bits of hair sticking to Drew's tearstained face, we thought, "Maybe next time will go better . . . surely, it must."

6
Our Genius Son

When Drew was nineteen months old, I became pregnant for the second time. I had a real purpose in getting pregnant this time: Drew desperately needed a friend and playmate. He needed to learn that he was not the only person in the world. David and I beamed with happiness upon learning of my pregnancy.

Despite my faithfulness at exercise, I gained weight at a rapid speed. On one of my gynecological visits I got miffed at the chubby nurse.

"Maybe we should cut back on the sweet rolls for breakfast," she chirped.

"Maybe you should watch your own caloric intake," I muttered to myself, climbing down off of the scale.

Though I tried to keep my weight down, it escalated at a rapid pace. I figured, then, that if I was going to blimp out no matter what, I might as well enjoy my food.

One of my favorite places to go was the Country Harvest Buffet. David was sure they lost money when I ate there, with my eating-for-two–sized portions. I would push past David and Drew to get to the head of the line. Even the mashed potatoes, dumped from an industrial-sized can and heated under the lights, appealed to me.

Another good thing about eating at the buffet was the atmosphere. It was very calming. We soon realized it was because the ceiling above us was dotted with spinning fans. Drew would quickly become mesmerized by the action above him.

What a perfect place to eat in peace, I thought. *Drew is happy, and so am I.*

I was especially hungry one evening and looking forward to the meal. After ambling past my family with my waddling gait, I found a perfect spot to plant the family. We always found a place near the food so that access wouldn't be difficult. All seemed well until, for no reason at all, Drew broke out into his usual freak-out cry.

What could it be this time? I went into my Nancy Drew mystery sleuth mode. *Maybe it's where we chose to sit, or maybe it's the color of the sippy cup I produced out of the diaper bag, or maybe . . .* My mind raced to come up with the problem. Finally, I saw it.

Above us, near our table, a fan and light were out of commission. The fan was still, the bulb dark. Out of all the whirling fans above us, that particular one made Drew desperate because it wasn't working. No explanation we could give would suffice to squelch Drew's apparent dismay over the glaring mechanical failure.

"Look at this one over here, honey. It's spinning nice and fast!"

Drew screamed, knocking silverware to the floor.

Eventually David and I had to inhale our food, gather our things, and leave.

Once in the car, Drew was quiet and acted as if nothing had ever happened. Why was such an incidental thing so important to our little boy? My nerves were shot and I was short of breath from our escape to the parking lot. I was still hungry. David went through the Dairy Queen drive-thru to make up for all that I had missed because of Drew's hysterics. At that moment in time, adding another child to the mix looked overwhelming. How could we possibly ever go anywhere as a family? We were all being taken hostage because of one child's fear.

It became obvious that, with our growing family, we needed more space. A few months before I gave birth, we moved to a house with three bedrooms and a tiny yard. We began making plans for the coming infant by fixing up a nursery across the hall from our room. Drew would have his own room.

Not long after we moved, Drew was moved into a twin bed and the crib went to the nursery. Because Drew had only known to wait for us to come and get him out of bed, the transition from crib to bed was a breeze. Without our even telling him to, he remained on his bed every morning and waited to be gotten up. The foot of his bed was stacked with books and Matchbox cars for when he woke up. Sometimes I would hear him playing for hours before he fell asleep and then again early in the morning upon waking. It didn't bother us that he didn't sleep the whole time as long as he was quiet and stayed on his bed. The windowsill over his bed became his own little parking lot and road on which his cars would travel back and forth endlessly. The main difficulty we experienced with the transition was his apparent obsession with the mini-blinds over the window.

Titch, titch, titch, titch, titch, titch. Drew found it fascinating to move the blinds so that they would swing and rhythmically bang against the window. The unrelenting tapping was driving me mad. I could hear it no matter where I was in the house, no matter what I was doing.

Titch, titch, titch, titch, on and on they swung.

Drew didn't even seem to notice that I was talking to him when I asked him to please stop. He was lost in his own little world, doing his own thing. The only remedy I could think of was to just keep the blinds elevated any time he was on his bed. It worked. It was as if he forgot about them when he didn't see them.

Since Drew had such a love for vehicles, I was happy he could view the street in front of our house from his bed. He could keep track of the whole neighborhood traveling by. The fact that he didn't know any of our neighbors and had no emotional connection to them made it difficult to understand his display of feelings every time the neighbors across the street drove off to work in the morning. Predictably at 7:40 A.M. every Monday through Friday screams of terror would emanate from Drew's room.

What could possibly be wrong with him? I would wonder, stumbling to his room. Upon entering his room, I would be met with the same scene every morning: little Drew, kneeling on his bed, gripping the sill and screaming at the window. When the cars would disappear from view, he would stop.

47

"You need to get self-control," I would say. "There is no reason to carry on like this."

My words seemed to float down the street behind the cars. I had no effect on his behavior. Leaving his room, I would hear him settle down eventually and play with his cars on the windowsill.

Around this same time, Drew said his first words. He was almost two and a half. "Ock" for "clock" was his first spoken word. We thought this rather humorous because he had always been on a schedule. Then came the recitations of license plate numbers.

"435, 612, 214, 976"

The mere sound of a familiar vehicle passing in front of our house would prompt him to recite its license plate number. I would run and check, just to see, and sure enough, he was always right.

Eventually his vocabulary included only single words—all nouns, and now the numbers. It was as if we had finally made contact. Minimal as it was, we had still made contact. Drew wouldn't look us in the eyes to communicate, but most of the time he would answer our question if we asked, "What is this?" and pointed to a chair, ball, book, cup, etc. He offered the numbers of cars without request. They just came bubbling out for whoever was interested.

We didn't realize the depth of Drew's obsession with numbers until one evening after church when he was at his post on the front steps. We heard him say every license plate number of every car that was leaving. He was always right. Standing every week on the steps of the church had become more than just a love for watching wheels; it was an exercise of phenomenal memory skills.

For the first time, David and I began to think that we had a very special child.

"He must be a genius!" I exclaimed to David one evening at home. "All you have to do is ask him the number of the red truck or the blue car, and he'll give me the correct answer!"

David and I had fun going down the list of cars, vans, and trucks that parked at church every week, and asking Drew for their numbers. Drew was never wrong and he never took long to respond to our number questions.

"Oh, David, what if he really is a genius!"

I was so happy to finally be able to take some parental pride in something Drew did. It was always painfully obvious to me while at church or with friends that my son wasn't the one that attracted affection. He just didn't draw you to himself. People didn't even want to dare try a "hello" out on him, for fear he might go berserk in their face. Now, at least we could say with confidence, "He may not be very lovable, but at least he's smart!"

Our excitement over his amazing intellect was piqued when, without noticing it much at first, I realized that it was the alphabet he was reciting one day. Sitting on the couch reading, I spotted Drew on the floor with some of his library books spread out around him. This activity wasn't unusual for Drew, except for the fact that he was pointing to each page of his book and mumbling something. I stopped my reading to listen more carefully, for I had never seen Drew notice the pages with such intensity before. My excitement was hard to contain as I waited for him to get to the letter Z. I flipped out and ran over to him when he finished.

"Wow! What a good job, honey. You said all of your letters. Daddy will be so happy!" I exclaimed.

I cheered for Drew and reached for him, but he just tried to scamper away from me. I didn't even care.

"You go on and play, sweetie. Save your brain power to show Daddy tonight," I called to his back as he retreated to his room.

I went back to my spot on the couch with a feeling of euphoria. *My little boy knows the alphabet! All of those hours of reading to him, and I had no clue anything was actually getting through!*

About the same time, just after turning two, Drew became intrigued with digital clocks. We liked to impress people with his ability to tell time and did it once at a friend's house.

"Drew, what are the numbers on the clock?" I asked.

Running to the oven, he would announce with confidence, "Three twenty-five."

"Wow! My daughter doesn't even know her numbers from one to ten yet!" exclaimed a mother whose girl was several months older than Drew.

My heart swelled with pride at this seemingly above-average ability my son displayed with perfect exactness. Drew had something that made him stand out in a good way for once, and you can be sure we didn't try to hide it.

Then it came. The all-too-familiar scream, blasting from the kitchen.

"AAAHHHHHHHH," cried Drew.

Everybody rushed into the kitchen together. Since I was adept at figuring Drew out, it was obvious to me what the matter was.

"Why, just look, anyone can see that the clock on the oven is two minutes faster than the clock on the microwave," I explained, pointing to the appliances.

Drew's screams resounded through the room as everyone looked on in silence, confusion painted on their faces. Somehow, trying to make sense out of the senseless was only beginning to make me look neurotic myself.

7
Mavis Beacon Teaches Typing

One warm, perfectly clear summer afternoon we decided to take Drew to the park. We didn't live far from Point Defiance, one of the most beautiful parks in the Northwest. But as we dressed Drew in shorts and a sleeveless shirt, he began to cry.

"Why do you have to make everything so difficult?" I said, exhausted.

Drew seemed deaf to my words and grew increasingly agitated over the clothing. Not having worn shorts yet that summer, he seemed totally baffled by their presence on his body. He kept pulling at the legs in hopes—we could only guess—of lengthening them to where he felt they should be. All the while he was working himself up into an anxiety attack. This lack of self-control was not acceptable behavior to David and me. What we wanted to hear was a "Yes, Mommy" in response to my telling him he had to wear the shorts. He paid no attention to me as he worked on his pant legs.

"No fussing! You need to get self-control," and with that he was corrected.

This made Drew angry and not at all remorseful. His wails increased in intensity.

"Mommy said no fussing!"

He received the same consequence once again. This did get his attention and he gradually quieted down when placed on his bed and left alone in his room.

Our anticipation over going to the park for the afternoon was dwindling, especially when the same scenario was immediately played out again when I put the "never-seen-before" sandals on his feet. After hearing Drew quiet himself again, I entered his room to get him and put him in the carseat. His face was red and blotchy from crying. Sitting on his bed, I reached for him to hold him for a minute before

51

leaving. I wanted him to know that everything was okay and that I loved him, but he made his usual plunge away from my affection.

"Maybe not now, little guy, but you'll want it someday and my arms will still be here to give it," I whispered to him.

We left for the park, already tired from the effort it had taken just to get out the door. Drew had, at least, learned that getting out of control was unacceptable—no matter what the problem was. But I felt empty because of the lack of resolution. I hadn't a clue how Drew felt.

Because Drew seemed to have a willful, hard heart, David and I frequently prayed that he would learn to obey with a good attitude. We could only try our best to remain faithful in our responsibility to train him. It was the most exhausting test of patience we had ever experienced.

When we arrived at the park, we found a secluded spot to spread out our blanket. I sat down on the blanket to watch David make an attempt to play some ball with his boy.

This ought to be good, I thought.

David carried Drew from our car to the grass and put him down to run, but his feet remained firmly planted where they were, as if stuck in cement.

"C'mon, Drew," shouted David as he kicked the soccer ball.

Drew just stood there looking down at those despicable sandals, as if they were preventing him from moving. David tried to tempt Drew again with the ball. It bumped him and rolled a few feet from where Drew was standing. Thinking the urge to retrieve the ball would be great enough to get him moving, I yelled, "Go on and get the ball, honey!"

Drew remained immovable. We realized it was a combination of things that was keeping him from playing. Not only did the sandals not feel right to him, but the grass, tickling his toes, was too much to bear. After a few more attempts at enticing the statue, David gave up and, swooping Drew up, placed him on the blanket next to me. Drew seemed to relax next to me, even though he still had to wear those horrid sandals.

To be sure of himself, Drew reached out and touched the grass with his hand. Recoiling, he acted as if he had just touched needles.

"How odd you are! Children like to play in the grass," I smiled at him.

Drew appeared nervous and stiff as he sat motionless next to me. He returned no smile, but looked seriously ahead to where the cars were parking in a lot, off in the distance. We all sat quietly for a long time, watching the cars cruise by. The only way to be happy, it seemed, was to enter his world with him.

Drew's frustration fits grew to be the norm between his second and third years. I tried to handle them the best I knew how. Whenever he lost control over something—cars not lining up just so, or clothes he had to wear, or an activity I was changing, or whatever—his behavior met the same consequence each time. "No fussy—you need to get self-control," I said, correcting him. Disciplining him seemed the only way to actually get his attention.

Despite Drew's inability to talk very well, he was still taught the proper way to respond to us: "Yes, Mommy." I always gave him some time alone on his bed to calm down. It really seemed to help to give him private time to settle himself after we disciplined him. We always tried to reconcile with him when he had calmed down . . . but he never wanted it. I kept up this response to Drew's fits for a full year before I actually saw some fruit for my labor. It was a very long year, but the Lord eventually blessed our efforts.

When I was eight months pregnant, I had an ultrasound performed. We had gotten an ultrasound when I was pregnant with Drew, too. The difference in the two ultrasounds was astounding. Drew had been fidgety and jerky. He had crossed and uncrossed his legs so that we weren't able to detect his sex. In comparison to this second pregnancy, Drew had reminded me of *The Karate Kid*. The baby I now carried seemed so relaxed. It was no mystery, according to the ultrasound, that we were going to have another boy. We had wanted another boy—a brother for Drew. David kissed my hand and we cried as we watched Drew's brother wave his tiny hand on the screen. It wouldn't be long now.

❖ ❖ ❖

Drew had always loved music, that is, music played on a radio or CD player. He seemed to prefer classical or anything with an orderly rhythm. What made listening to music most enjoyable for him was to be able to rock in the rocking chair and watch the numbers changing on the CD player. He appeared so perfectly happy during these music-rocking-watching-the-numbers sessions that we made it a point to indulge him daily with this treat. It made us so happy to see him take such pleasure in something for a change.

When David's boss installed a new computer system, we were offered the company's old computer and printer. Even though this foreign-looking object was accepted into our home, neither of us knew the first thing about how to use it. Convinced that our son was a budding genius, we knew a computer was the perfect thing to help him along in his intellectual pursuits. We decided the computer would be Drew's and would be set up in his room. Perhaps he would eventually teach us how to use this highly technical apparatus.

In the pile of computer paraphernalia that came to live with us was a disk on learning to type: Mavis Beacon Teaches Typing. This soon became Drew's new obsession. What more could a boy who loved letters and numbers, as he did, ask for in this life?

After figuring out how to plug the equipment in, David tried the typing disk. Voilà! The computer screen lit up with a picture of a keyboard. Drew was in ecstasy.

"Ohhhh," he blinked in amazement.

It didn't take him long to learn the location of all of the letters on the keyboard and try some of the typing exercises. One of his favorite things to do was to turn on the metronome for the timed typing exercise and watch it "blip," then mount his rocking horse to gaze at the screen, transfixed. Drew would rock back and forth, his eyes never leaving the screen before him. He had a look of immense pleasure.

He practiced more and more, and after several months he became so proficient at typing he had made it up to 35 wpm. I would get an eerie feeling whenever I passed his room. Glancing in at him, I would be taken aback by what I saw. With the glow of the computer screen casting a greenness on his face, he resembled a mad scientist at work. His eyes were bright and intense, yet his face didn't register any particular emotion. Knowing Drew, I would call him happy at that moment. But only because he wasn't crying.

One evening I went into the kitchen to prepare supper. Something made me stop short as I reached out to open the refrigerator door. All of Drew's multi-colored magnetic letters on the refrigerator were arranged in perfect order . . . not of the alphabet, but of the keyboard on his computer.

8
The New Addition

My second pregnancy was much different from the first. I felt miserable most of the time, fatigued, irritable, spent. Because of my size, I was unable to clean and fix up our new house. That, combined with Drew's now-constant negative behavior and my discomfort, pushed me into a chronic depression. I looked around at my new house and only saw a million things which needed to be done: cupboards to clean, boxes to unpack, lost order to be found.

Because Drew was still on a routine, our lives didn't completely fall apart. When I wasn't reading to him or playing with him, I was camped out on the couch. I could barely move and I was always fatigued. Trying to get some rest one day and feeling my most miserable, I heard the now all-too-familiar scream-cry coming from Drew's room. Heaving myself up off the couch to deal with Drew's outburst, I felt overwhelmed with life. I entered Drew's room with very little patience. Without even trying to figure out what the problem was, I dealt with him exactly the way I had for many months now.

"No fussy. You need to get self-control!"

He was disciplined and then placed on his bed to quiet himself. Before leaving his room, I turned toward the still-screaming Drew and yelled, "What is the matter with you? Why can't you just stop screaming?"

With that I turned and left him, slamming the door behind me. My guilty tears burned my eyes as I managed to make it back to my spot on the couch. I buried my tired face in my hands as Drew's screams remained strong and echoed in my head.

"Please help me, God," I moaned. "I just don't have the strength to deal with him today."

The faraway screams eventually died out. I sat and waited. I knew all too well they would be back again.

56

❖ ❖ ❖

Finally the day came when my water broke and we were going to experience childbirth yet again. It was New Year's morning and we had arranged for Drew to be cared for by a friend while I was at the hospital. My friend's husband arrived early in the morning to pick up an unsuspecting Drew. The whole idea of leaving him overnight with someone else was not one that gave me any comfort. But what could we do? I had to leave him. All I could do now was remain focused so that I could deal with the contractions.

The knock at the door made me jump. Everything was packed for Drew to spend the night away from home—this would be his first. He was just over two years old and still there was no communication of any sort nor any eye contact. David loaded Drew's belongings into our friends' car and then came back for Drew. I was doing my best to remain strong for Drew's sake. After aiming a kiss at Drew's cheek that was intercepted by a swift turn of his head, I watched David go out the door with him. Counting the minutes between contractions, I heard Drew's blood-curdling scream echo throughout the neighborhood. I peeked out the window and saw two grown men struggling to put a small boy into the backseat of a car.

"Ohhhhh," I groaned as a contraction hit. Sitting down again, I began to sweat and tense up at Drew's continuing screams. When the next contraction came, I tried to relax. *We are just beginning,* I thought. *We aren't even to the hospital yet. I just need to concentrate on relaxing—there simply isn't anything I can do about Drew.*

After what seemed to be an eternity, the sound of Drew's cries ended with the slam of a car door. A moment later David returned looking pale.

"What was going on out there? You probably woke the whole neighborhood!" I grimaced with the next contraction.

"He just started to freak out when I tried to put him in a different car than he was used to."

57

A small thing like that was all it took to set Drew off. Now all we could do was try to put him out of our minds the best we could and get this baby delivered. We could only hope that our friends would still be our friends when the ordeal was over.

After checking in at the hospital and having it determined that "Yes, you are really pregnant and not just overweight" and "Yes, you really are in labor; you need to stay," I settled on the bed in the maternity ward. My mind immediately went to Drew. I wondered how he was doing, if he had screamed the whole way in the car and if he was still screaming now. David made a call to our friends' house to check. Using the phone by my bed, I received the report that all was well. I didn't mind at all if she was lying to me—what could I possibly do about it anyway? We called frequently and received the same report over the next several hours. Her reassuring voice helped me to concentrate on relaxing for the contractions. I didn't have any room in my head to worry about Drew—not now.

It was a Sunday, the day of rest, when I went into labor. I couldn't believe that things could go so smoothly, but they did. I received an epidural in plenty of time so that I didn't suffer at all. Making jokes with the hospital staff, I pushed a tiny person out of my body and into the hands of the doctor. It was a jovial scene in that dim room. All had gone well and I thanked God for blessing David and me once again with a son, Drew's brother.

Crying tears of joy, I held my baby's limp, warm body next to mine. How precious life is. David happily kissed my lips over and over as I cried and clutched our new son. He felt so relaxed and helpless next to my pounding heart. Mindful of the difficult experience mothering had been for me so far, I reveled in this completely calm, immobile creature, drinking in this moment of bliss. I knew all too well what lay ahead.

I was so excited I couldn't sleep at all that first night in the hospital. I desperately wanted to get home and all together as a family. As I lay there, I could see David's peaceful body, sound asleep in the recliner. My mind wandered to Drew.

I wonder how peaceful things are with him and our friends.
I worried more about Drew than I missed him. This thought made
me feel terribly guilty.

I couldn't get out of the hospital soon enough the following day. I
was anxious to see Drew and watch his response to his new brother.
Elliot Jon Steere rode quietly in the infant carseat behind us. A receiving blanket covered with bears was thrown over him to shield his sweet
face from the harsh glare of the sun.

"Can't you go any faster?" I nagged.

"I'm going the speed limit," David countered.

After what seemed like a cross-country trip, we finally pulled into
the driveway of our friends' house. Because I was beginning to feel a bit
sore, I remained in the car with Elliot while David went to the door. I
was more tense than when we drove to the hospital to have the baby.
Staring at the front door of the house, I waited impatiently for David
and Drew. Finally, everybody emerged with no visible signs of distress.
I relaxed somewhat, until I remembered my appearance. Not having
remembered to bring even my comb or toothbrush with me to the hospital because of my concentration on Drew's well-being, I could imagine what a disheveled mess I must be. I thanked our friends profusely
for all that they had done for us. Drew came around to my side of the
car and David encouraged, "Give Mommy a hug, Drew!"

Knowing my limits in pushing my affection on him, I reached out
to Drew and waited for some sign from him that it would be acceptable
to hug him. I actually thought I saw a hint of desire for me in his eyes.
His face wore its usual serious look as David swung him into my lap,
but I was sure I saw him reach out to me ever so slightly. The "hug"
lasted a mere second, then David buckled Drew into his carseat behind
me. As we drove home I watched Drew to see his response to Elliot's
presence with us. Elliot gurgled and moved the receiving blanket. This
startled Drew but his interest was fleeting. After a short, anticlimactic
glance at this new human life next to him, he returned his attention to
the cars zipping past his window. Nothing else.

Drew's lack of interest in his new brother continued when we arrived home. Neither David nor I believed we should make a big deal of this, but chose, rather, to let Drew become involved on his own timetable. Over the next months Drew remained ambivalent toward the new member of the family. The only time he really showed any notice of him was when Elliot cried. Drew would instantly begin to scream and cry, too. Knowing it wasn't my attention he was after—it never was—I tried to figure out a reason for all of the carrying on. The only thing I could gather from the way he acted was that Elliot's cries perhaps actually hurt his ears.

While I was unpacking some baby items on the floor one day, Drew happened to be drawn to a soft, furry teddy bear. It was all white except for a red satin ribbon around its neck. I had received it as a gift when Drew was born, but he had never shown any interest in cuddly things. I was happy to see him become interested in something other than a car or truck, so I gladly handed it to him to play with. From the moment he got it, it never left his side. We soon had to establish some boundaries concerning Bear. Bear would sit in the corner of the kitchen while Drew ate, and he would stay on Drew's bed if we ever went anywhere away from home. These rules, like any we made, were met with wails and tears. "No fussy. You need to say, 'Yes, Mommy.' " I would correct him and then give him some time on his bed to settle himself down. I would always make an attempt at restoration but was still met with the same fleeing Drew.

Over time, once a pattern was set for any particular routine, Drew would come to accept it. If we should happen to change it for any reason, he would lose control. One area in which this could be seen was in Drew's bedtime rituals. David or I would have to make a quick glance around his room before closing his door for the night. "Is the closet door closed? Does he have Bear on his bed? Are the mini-blinds up? Does he have an ample supply of cars on his windowsill? Is there a pile of books at the foot of his bed?" You can be sure that if something was not "right," his cries would be heard within moments of our leaving the room.

We would never try to provoke Drew if we knew how he expected something to be done, but at the same time, we didn't give in to or accommodate him if he lost control over something after we had said to do it a certain way. We felt we had to train him to obey readily and happily despite his apparent distress over the situation. Correction was always dealt if Drew cried when given instructions, even over matters as insignificant as where and how Bear was placed in the corner of the kitchen before Drew sat down at the table to eat. He had to learn to get control over his spirit—how could he survive this life if he didn't?

Having learned to recognize the letters of the alphabet, Drew became bored when I went over them again and again in his books. I decided the next step was to teach him the sounds of the letters. David and I had always planned on home schooling our children, but I never dreamed I would have to actually start when Drew was only two and a half. I wasn't trying to push him—I felt like I was trying to keep up with him.

I ended up making flash cards of all of the letters and keeping them in a three-ring binder. A ten-minute session of phonics, twice a day, was now added to our schedule. Within a two-month period, Drew had all of the sounds down. At this point, on a huge piece of paper I wrote out a series of three- and four-lettered words. I didn't require Drew to perform, but, rather, I just demonstrated to him how to sound out the words using the sounds he had just learned. This became a daily activity so that by the time Drew was three he could easily read about forty small words. He got the hang of it very quickly as he watched me slowly pronounce every sound as I pointed to it. When it was obvious he was bored, I had him sound them out. New words were added to the list daily.

Drew still didn't make eye contact and seemed to prefer being left alone. He remained stiff in appearance and anxious in temperament. He only tolerated any activity I engaged him in and never appeared to really enjoy life. Elliot, on the other hand, was everything Drew wasn't. He was a joy to care for and live with. We put him on a routine at birth just as we had with Drew. Breastfeeding wasn't the trial it had been with Drew. I chalked it up to being more relaxed as a second-time mom.

Elliot slept well and was completely relaxed. He was sleeping through the night by six weeks. He took after my side of the family with his fair skin and hair, and he wasn't as big and robust as Drew had been. We grew to love him more each day. Almost from the first time we laid eyes on Elliot, we sensed a knowing look in his eyes. He would stare right into my eyes with such a peaceful and happy expression—I was certain there was something very wrong with him. He just looked too wise for his years with his obvious calm understanding.

"Maybe Elliot is a genius, too," I mused with delight. "Is it possible to have two?"

Despite Elliot's desire for Drew as he tracked him with his eyes, Drew remained aloof and unmoved.

It was a sunny day and things were going quite well. Drew was sitting quietly eating his sandwich and I was feeding Elliot some rice cereal as he sat in an infant seat placed on the table. Suddenly the doorbell startled all of us. Not knowing who it could possibly be, I yelled, "Who is it?"

"It's your neighbor from across the street," came the reply.

I opened the door a little anxiously because I had not met any of our neighbors yet and wondered what she could want.

"Could I please trouble you and ask you to put this ice cream cake in the refrigerator?" she asked with a begging expression, handing me a white box.

"Of course, c'mon in," I said, taking the box and going to the kitchen.

I was relieved that this was all it was about and not a complaint about screams she could most likely hear coming from our house.

"My husband," she said, "was supposed to have our locks fixed by today. Can you believe this? I'm throwing a birthday party in an hour and I went to pick up the cake. When I came home I found out that my key won't work in the lock. Would you mind if I used your phone to call my husband?"

She was instantly cut off by Drew's piercing scream. It had been a long time since I had seen Drew this desperate. He began thrashing and screaming, knocking his plate and sippy cup off the table while strapped in his booster chair. The simple unannounced entrance of this alien into our home had sent Drew out of control.

Pointing my neighbor in the direction of the phone, I whisked Drew out of his chair and put him in his room on his bed. My face was red with embarrassment when I appeared back in the kitchen. Drew's screams could still be heard through the walls.

"I apologize for all of that," I mumbled, wet with perspiration.

"Oh, forget it," she said while she finished dialing the phone.

Despite her relaxed response to Drew's outburst, I was angry with Drew for making me look so bad in front of my neighbor whom I was meeting for the first time. *What must she think of me, with such an out-of-control child!*

Her husband showed up within minutes and my neighbor left with her cake. Still trembling, I entered Drew's room. Drew sat in the same spot where I had left him. Although he was much calmer now, he made little gaspy noises when he inhaled, and his face was wet and blotchy. I approached him with clear determination.

"You were very fussy—that was a bad attitude." I disciplined him. This brought more tears. I left Drew on his bed to calm down and went back to Elliot, who had found the rag and was patiently and contentedly sucking on it.

"Hi, sweetie," I whispered.

Elliot beamed at me.

I began to cry.

9
For the Love of Bear

For his second birthday Drew had been given a wooden puzzle of numbers by a friend. He had always liked it, and one of his favorite pastimes with it was to use the pieces to make three- and four-digit numbers.

One day, while passing his room, I glanced in and found him at the number 2093. He carefully placed the numbers on the carpet. I watched as he then removed the number 3 and replaced it with the number 4. Then from the number 4 came the switch to the number 5. He faithfully continued this work until he reached the number 2100, borrowing some numbers from another puzzle. Thinking he was probably bored with this, I turned to go. I stopped short, though, when I noticed him begin to do the count backward: "2099" read the new computation on the floor. Then 2098, 2097, 2096, etc.

This ability to count in the thousands was transferred over to the finding of hymns as they were announced at church. We sang from a hymnal that had hymn numbers into the thousands. Drew listened for the numbers to be announced and BANG, he was off to find it as fast as he could. This was the only time he seemed to be aware of what was going on around him at church. The announcement of numbers jarred him into action. When he found the hymn, his face wore a look of satisfaction.

"Good job, Drew," David whispered, patting him on the back.

The singing of hymns became a tolerable activity when Drew could participate in his own special way.

When we were at someone else's home, it was clearly an obsession of Drew's to find the heater vents, light switches, and doors. Touching a light switch or a door knob had always been off limits at our house. It was evident from the way he acted away from home that this boundary was a wise one to have established. Being somewhere besides home gave Drew the idea that the "law" of touching was suddenly void. Whenever we were invited to somebody's home, it became a full-time job to watch Drew so that he wouldn't run up the electricity bill by playing with the light switch, or pinch someone's fingers in the door.

At church Drew became enamored with the heater vents and would gravitate toward them as soon as the service ended. He would lay his face on top of it to feel the heat blow out and tenderly run his fingers over the grate. We thought that his future held a promising position as a mechanic like his father. He never noticed people unless they bothered him somehow, and he could be bothered by just a simple hello.

When Drew was three years old, David's parents made their yearly trek out to Washington from Illinois. Drew had never taken any interest in his grandparents and, just as with everybody else, he acted as if they didn't exist. We thought that since Drew was a little older now, things would be different this year.

David took Drew to pick up his parents one evening from his sister's house who lived here in town. I stayed home with Elliot. When David's car pulled into our driveway, I went to the door to greet them. It was a somber group that emerged from our car. David pushed past me with a sullen face followed by a very quiet mother and father.

"What's wrong?" I pressed David for an explanation privately in the kitchen.

"Drew screamed the whole way home," replied David.

"Not only that," said David's mom, entering the kitchen, "he kicked at my leg the whole way over."

Drew had run to his room and was obviously over it now.

"I'm terribly sorry for Drew's behavior," I apologized with embarrassment.

This was not a good beginning to our visit with David's parents. Things did not improve when, at church the following Sunday, David's mom requested a family picture since everybody looked their best.

We separated from the crowd at church and moved toward a secluded area in the back of the parking lot where there were some trees. The closer we got, the more anxious Drew became. Soon he was screaming with terror and clamoring to escape from David's strong arms. All I could think of was that we had never before traveled to this strange place and that it made Drew mad with fear. Our words of explanation were drowned out by shrieks and wails. Drew had no idea what was going on.

We tried to hurriedly group up for a photo and be done with it, but Drew just wouldn't settle down. There was no picture taken that day—I was somewhat happy about that because it would have been a moment I wanted to forget anyway.

Whenever we attempted to get a picture of Drew, even in the safety of his own home, the picture almost never turned out. Every time the shutter clicked, Drew squeezed his eyes shut.

"Why does he always close his eyes?" questioned David's mom. "Why should he be afraid of the flash?"

We had no answer. Even if the pictures were taken out doors, with no flash, Drew inevitably closed his eyes for fear of it. Nothing could persuade him to smile and open his eyes when we wanted to take a picture. Nearly every picture we ever got of him is one with a grimacing face and closed eyes.

When David's parents returned home, the holidays were approaching; it was time to visit my parents. Even though they lived nearby, we rarely saw them because we had to travel by ferry to the island where they lived.

We drove our car onto the ferry and, once parked, got out of the car to go upstairs and sit in the warmth for the duration of the half-hour trip. We all piled onto the elevator with David holding Elliot and me holding Drew's hand. Once the dreaded doors closed and the movement began, I remembered why we never used elevators. Drew began to scream his fiercest. I reached down to pick him up in an attempt to comfort him—even though I knew it wouldn't work. It never had before. Faster than a speeding bullet, Drew was pulling at my coat and screaming at top pitch right in my ear. The seconds it took to reach the next floor seemed like minutes. When the doors of the elevator finally opened, the scene which greeted the other travelers must have been an interesting sight, judging by the looks on their faces. Elliot was looking with grave concern at Drew; David began looking down at the floor when he saw the crowd staring at us; and Drew was still screaming as I awkwardly hiked him up onto my hip.

There was a group of passengers seated at a booth just inside the door. They were all quiet and looked at the opened elevator with serious expressions. We had the option of just letting the doors close again and going back to our car, or we could face the crowd with dignity. We chose the latter and hopped out just before the doors started to close behind us.

"He's just very afraid of elevators," I explained to the silent onlookers.

I tried to gracefully let Drew slide back to the floor and we all found a booth away from the rest of the people. Even after Drew settled down somewhat, it was a few more moments and a few more glances our way before conversations resumed to where they had left off before our arrival.

To avoid further trouble, we decided to take the stairs back down to our car when the ferry reached the shore. David and I made a distinct mental note to never, ever take an elevator again if we could possibly help it. It was a luxury we all could do without.

Secretly, over some time, I had begun to dread going into Drew's room to get him up for the day. At the same time, though, I couldn't wait to get Elliot. Of course I felt guilty for feeling this way about the two boys, but I couldn't see how I could help it. Elliot was such a dear, relaxed, happy child, and Drew was so very difficult. Within minutes of entering Drew's room, I would be met with a bad attitude that had to be dealt with. The second I started to dress him or tell him that it was time to eat breakfast, I inevitably met a cry of disapproval.

No matter how tired of dealing with Drew I was, however, I knew that if I ever let anything slide, it would certainly push us over the edge. We were at least maintaining some control; one lax moment would be too hard to make up for. We tried to be as consistent as possible and deal with Drew by training him to a standard of self-control. There was just no other choice.

It was odd, but Drew seemed to be in love with Bear—the one I had given him when unpacking the baby box. Bear was the only thing Drew actually showed some human emotions toward. He showed more concern and love for that inanimate object than he did for either David or me. Bear was constantly with him when we were at home. Drew was so unnaturally attached that even taking Bear from him for the purpose of washing him was a traumatic experience.

This traumatic experience occurred the day Bear got really dirty. One day I smelled an all too familiar odor emanating from Drew's room. His pants were in need of an immediate diaper change. Laying Drew on the changing pad, I undid his diaper and exposed the mess. Quick as a flash, Drew grabbed his side kick, Bear, and without meaning to, managed to flick Bear's left paw into the soiled area. I grabbed Bear to keep his destruction to a minimum. Drew freaked out and acted as though he thought he would never see his beloved Bear again.

After finishing Drew's diaper change, I took Bear and impatiently threw him into the washing machine with some other dirty laundry. The look on Drew's face was unforgettable. He screamed with distress as Bear was plunged into the deep abyss. Drew acted as though Bear had been thrown into Hades for eternity. I slammed the machine shut and it began its cycle of swishing. The last glimpse of Bear I caught before closing him in, mixed with the terror I saw on Drew's face, made me think of a line from the book *The Velveteen Rabbit*: "I *am* real . . . the boy himself said so."

Despite my efforts to console Drew, he cried fiercely for the entire wash cycle. When Bear was extracted from the washer and thrown into the dryer, Drew became even more hysterical.

When Bear was handed back to Drew, all warm and clean from the dryer, Drew was instantly euphoric. He grabbed Bear and rubbed him all over his face as if to kiss him.

With a wistful sigh I thought, *How I wish he loved me that much.*

10
Echoes in the Wind

We had decided to not try potty training Drew until after Elliot was on a pretty predictable routine. That time came when Drew was about two and a half. Some of my friends had potty trained their eighteen-month-old girls. This was unbelievable to me. Drew seemed so distractible and verbally unresponsive that even by two and a half the training seemed too soon. With two children in diapers, though, the thought of getting one out of them was strong motivation to try. Our plan was to stay positive about it and not become negative unless we had clear indication that Drew was being willful about not using the toilet when we knew he was able. So we began. Our idea was to take Drew to the toilet on somewhat of a routine, and if he should happen to go, we would praise him profusely and give him a tangible reward; in his case this would be a Skittle. If he didn't go in the toilet but soiled his diaper, we wouldn't say anything about it.

We began taking him when we got him up in the morning, before and after meals, and before and after naps, then again before bed at night. We did this for several days with no success. We knew it was impossible to try to get him to tell us when he needed to go—that seemed way over his head. Drew couldn't even tell us he was thirsty and wanted some juice. I couldn't imagine him requesting to use the toilet. Nevertheless, all of the baby books said that by two years old most children are able to begin potty training successfully.

The first day Drew urinated into the toilet was a triumphal day. Of course, he was not intending to do it; it just happened because of a sudden chill.

"Good job, Drew! You went potty in the toilet and not in your pants! You get a Skittle," I said, handing him a colored treat. Drew seemed baffled by the whole episode. I don't think he even realized what he had done.

We continued to take him to the bathroom on a schedule, but it remained hit-and-miss whether he performed or not. Even with all of the praise, it seemed he just didn't "get it." Though he appeared startled by our outbursts of praise, he readily took the Skittle. Over time we expected him to at least improve, but he remained unclear about what was expected of him when we pulled down his pants and positioned him in front of the toilet.

Without knowing how else to take it, by the time Drew was three, and then three and a half, David thought that he must just be acting obstinate.

"Maybe it's time to take stricter measures," said David. "We have been at this for some time now."

I thought the opposite. I just didn't think Drew understood. How could I discipline him for that? But I followed David's lead and corrected Drew the following day for wetting in his pants instead of the toilet. Crying, with confusion written all over his face, he mimicked my words: "Need to go in the toilet and not in your pants." This was his usual way of talking now—copying us.

That night I pleaded with David to just give it some more time. I was sure he would eventually "get it."

Having two children in diapers was not easy or fun for me. I really didn't know what we were doing wrong. I finally convinced David to continue with our old approach. I just could not penalize Drew for something he didn't even know he'd done. I already had enough to contend with just keeping him from spinning the toilet paper roll around and around and from losing control because there was no clean edge on the toilet paper.

"Oh nooo!" Drew would cry as he desperately tried to rip off any bits of paper that were keeping the edge from being neat.

"Just go potty, Drew," I said impatiently in his ear.

He was so distracted, it seemed a waste of time to keep trying, but we did it anyway, knowing that it had to happen someday. David and I couldn't think of any adults who were still in diapers; we were sure Drew would learn eventually. We persevered, however, even though we saw no end in sight.

When Drew was almost four years old, there was virtually no reciprocal conversation. If we asked Drew, "What did you do in Sunday school today?" he answered, "Do in Sunday school today." We could get no information from him.

"Drew, where is Bear?"

"Where is Bear?" he repeated.

Anything we ever questioned of him was just repeated to us. The fact that he was talking at all was good enough for us. We simply did not recognize his echoing of our questions as cause for concern.

It was a rainy, blustery day. David, Elliot, Drew, and I got into the car to travel to the grocery store for our weekly supply. I never went anywhere alone with the boys. I just did not feel capable of handling Drew alone in public because of his unpredictable nature. David and I were eventually going everywhere together.

Climbing out of the car in the grocery store parking lot, Drew became wild with agitation.

"Ohhhhhhh!" he cried, hiding his head in his arms. The wind was swirling and Drew acted terrorized by its blast.

Running sideways to protect his face, he screamed the whole way to the front doors of the store.

"Is it blowing on you?" he screeched. It was a common practice for Drew to put his statements in the form of a question as if he were speaking our lines to himself.

Pulling him by the hand, I tried to drag him out of the wind into the safety of the building. The wind continued to whip around his little body and face as he screamed even louder with fear.

Finally in the store, he calmed down a bit. David swung him into a cart and tried to wipe Drew's wet, cold face.

Drew spoke shakily, "Was it very hard?"

"Yes, sweetie, the wind was blowing very hard. Everything is okay now."

"Okay now," repeated Drew.

Putting my hand on his chest, I could feel his heart trying to beat its way out. This was certainly no joke with him. He was dead serious and nothing could help except to remove him from whatever it was that was terrorizing him. In this case, it was simply the wind.

11
The Monster Appears

Because of David's usual late work nights, it was an unusual evening in that he and I sat relaxing on the couch together halfheartedly watching TV. We were discussing our days and enjoying the lazy comfort of each other's company. Our conversation was interrupted by a popular news show, detailing the life of an adult autistic woman named Temple Grandin, who was promoting her book, *Thinking in Pictures*. Our interest was piqued when the woman began to describe herself as a child.

"The autistic child will go berserk over a cushion out of place on the couch."

Instantly, we recognized this very commonplace behavior that we had witnessed in Drew so many times. A sick feeling developed in the pit of my stomach as the woman continued to talk in a loud and stilted manner.

"My reaction to being touched was like a wild horse flinching and pulling away."

I stared at her and moved closer to the screen, not wanting to blink. I was glued to her every move and intent on her every word. Somehow, I knew that whatever was going to come out of this lady's mouth was something I needed to hear . . . something, though, that I didn't know if I could bear to hear.

"My hearing is like having a sound amplifier set on maximum loudness . . . " she continued.

My body wanted to run from the room with eyes shut tight and hands clasped over my ears, but it defied my secret will to run and I remained immovable where I was seated. I was forced to listen.

"By the time I was two and a half, my mother realized there was something dreadfully wrong; I had no speech and screamed constantly . . . ."

This flawless description of Drew—someone she had never even met—was beginning to make me panic. How could she so perfectly describe our son to us? These were more than just distinguishing marks of his personality.

"I had severe problems with anxiety, nervousness, and sensitivity to touch and sound. The anxiety felt like a constant state of stage fright for no reason . . . ."

The room began to feel warm . . . no, hot . . . very hot.

I reached to hold David's hand. We would be dragged together into this whirlwind which was quickly gathering momentum.

". . . Indicate that people with autism have structural abnormalities in the brain . . . ."

I wanted to yell at the TV, "Slow down!" The interview seemed to be traveling at top speed. My terrified mind was trying to keep up and process all that it was being blasted with.

"Did you hear what she said?" I whispered, not taking my eyes from the set despite the commercial which had just come on. Even though the mood on TV became instantly jovial, its sounds were muffled by the thick, foreboding atmosphere in the room. Turning to David, I couldn't miss the aching twist of his face as he stared blankly past me at the screen.

"Yeah," he mumbled.

We sat in silence waiting for the show to return from the commercial break. I leaned forward. My heart began to race wildly. Gripping each other's hand, we careened closer to the nightmare we so clearly saw aimed directly at us. The daunting description went on, striking us in the face, not caring a bit how it was affecting us.

". . . Rigid concrete thinking, no common sense, and lack of affect . . . due to sensory overload . . . ."

The impact was impolite, reckless, and terrifying. I felt shaken and sat quivering as though huddled in a corner with my arm shielding me from any more incoming blows. David remained with me.

"Autism is a disorder in which some parts of the brain are under-developed and other parts may be overdeveloped . . . ."

Will the blows ever stop? I wondered.

Despite my desperation for the attack to end, I couldn't help but peer fearfully over my protective arm.

More . . . give me more. If I have to have it, give it all to me! I thought to myself.

As the interview continued, the monster called autism took shape before our very eyes, and the paralyzing assault intensified with each detail given us.

The beautiful anchorwoman sat across from Temple Grandin and asked, "So, have you ever been in love?"

"Nope. Don't know anything about it! I never did understand Romeo and Juliet. I just didn't get it," she responded.

What kind of a person can't understand the most basic of human emotions? Is this the sum of all the horror we've been listening to—to be robbed of any ability to love? My thoughts tripped and tumbled over each other in an effort to understand this impossible idea. My thoughts fell headlong and crashed into Drew.

Numb with fear, I felt as though this monster now had me around the neck. I found it difficult to take a breath or even to swallow. Temple's words echoed in my head loud and clear, matching the rhythm of my heart. *Nope. Don't know anything about it . . . about it . . . about it.*

Tears finally managed to push their way out of my eyes, blurring my vision. Temple's words were like the prophetic words spoken by the "Ghost of Christmas future," only it wasn't Christmastime. A time of mirth wasn't being predicted, but rather death . . . a sudden and horrid death of someone you love with all of your heart. Drew's death.

Being overwhelmed, my mind tried desperately to cling to the moment. With so much information to process, I felt unable to take it all in at once. Slowly I melted out of reality for the balance of the show.

It was true—how could it not be? If Drew was autistic, it would certainly answer any question we had about the way he was. Switching off the set, I turned to David's arms. Without words, I knew David was thinking the very thoughts I was. We held each other in silence. I could feel David's heart pulsing with mine, sharing in the rhythm of terror mixed with sadness we both couldn't help but feel.

"He's autistic!" my mind reminded me every chance it got.

I couldn't go to bed that night or rise in the morning without hearing those words whispered in my mind just one more time. The absence of the son we thought we had became crystal clear the next morning. Drew's presence at the breakfast table was nothing out of the ordinary, but the distant look, echoing words, and anxious demeanor which characterized him caused us to look at him differently. No longer was he our dear boy with a fragile and sensitive personality, he was our autistic son with something dreadfully and profoundly unfixable in his brain. All of the screaming and anxiety, all of the desperate need for order and sameness, all of the detachment from the human race and, most importantly, from David and me, all of this impossible frustration had a term, its own name. Autism. It had been living with us for nearly four years; how could we have been so blind?

I couldn't get the autistic woman's words out of my mind: "Don't know anything about it . . . ." How awful to be on this earth and not have a clue about love. Not just a love for a future mate, but love in any sense. I couldn't keep myself from weeping—not so much for the love I didn't get from Drew, but more for the love he would never know he had from me.

My mind quickly went to the spiritual implications. If he couldn't even understand love for another creature, how could he ever love the living God whom he couldn't even see? I don't know any Christian parent who doesn't ponder the question of whether his or her child will be saved and who does not bring him before the Lord constantly. All of a sudden, this thought had new meaning for me. How could Drew ever be saved?

After thoughtful consideration, I knew the Scriptures enough to know that there wasn't hope for anyone apart from the grace of God. It takes the pure goodness of God to change anyone's heart to repent of their sins and to love Him.

Drew's salvation was no different from Elliot's—they both needed God's grace.

An indescribable ache and a sense of guilt began to suffocate me. How could I have been so cruel to him, so hasty to make assertions concerning his behavior, so pompous and overconfident in my role as parent? Now, all of our hard work in training Drew appeared shameful and abusive. How could I have been so harsh with him—he couldn't help it! This wrenching admission was almost more than I could take. Not only must I be the most ignorant mother to not have detected my son was autistic, but on top of that, I was guilty of being cruel to him. Would I have disciplined him for not seeing if he were blind?

From the moment the monster made its presence known, a dark cloak of grief enfolded me. Its intrusion was silent and insistent. Hardly realizing what was happening because of its subtle way, I sank unwittingly into the pit of despair. With every remembrance of another time I had unjustly treated Drew, I was silently coaxed and wooed, sinking softly, deeper and deeper.

A couple of days following the TV show, feeling stripped of all confidence as parents, David and I sat together on the couch and watched Drew rock in the rocking chair just as he had always done. He listened to the music and watched his precious numbers flick by. We both eyed him as if he was an intruder in our home—someone neither of us knew at all. Now what we once thought of as a happy gleam in his eyes while he rocked appeared eerie and strange. The stiff way he held himself and the loud voice that echoed our every statement back at us was a huge red flag slapping us in the face. How did we miss it?

In the following days the struggle to maintain daily life seemed enormous. Not only did I have a baby to care for, but Drew had needs greater than I knew how to handle. I cried constantly, by the bucket full, losing all equilibrium. The realization of Drew's obvious handicap was the first severing of a relationship in our home; the second breach was between David and me. A time of crisis brings out a person's true nature, as we soon learned. Being the two very different people that we are, the ways in which we grieved for our son were very different as well. David's natural make-up doesn't allow him to respond emotionally to anything. That's not to say he doesn't show his emotions, he's just not ruled by them. David's response to Drew was one of caring sympathy.

Late one evening a few nights after the emotional assault of the TV program, after watching Drew rock for some time in the rocking chair, David rose to get something to drink from the kitchen. Stopping for a moment in front of Drew's chair, David gently touched Drew's head and looked into his face as if he had just happened upon an injured animal. Not surprisingly, Drew jerked away from David's touch and appeared annoyed that the numbers were being blocked from his view. David showed me a look of pity for his son before he disappeared into the kitchen. My eyes became instantly crowded with tears.

Back and forth, back and forth, back and forth, Drew continued to rock, unmoved by the latest interaction between father and son.

Didn't Drew see how he just hurt his own father by rejecting his tender affection? There has to be something wrong with a child who continually rebuffs the ones who love him most. Witnessing this complete lostness of a person wearing this silent, empty face whisked me, once more, deeper into my pit of grief. *My precious son, my Drew.* I covered my face with my hands and sobbed.

Returning with his drink, David almost appeared annoyed with me. Since he didn't feel the need to lie on the couch and cry, he failed to see the sense in it when I did it.

"Don't you have any feelings for your son?" I yelled.

"Of course I do," he defended himself. "I just don't see what good it will do to lie there and cry about it all the time."

Well, that did it. Now I was alienated from both my son and, when I needed him most, my husband. How heartless and bold he seemed looming over me with disgust. Where were his tears, his pain, his struggle? I felt alone and surrounded by cold and blackness—as though screaming and gasping for my next breath. My heart was broken as I never dreamed possible, and the ache of helplessness seemed to be killing me.

The following day, unable to keep our nightmarish hunches to ourselves, I called Lorie Ann, a friend from church.

"I think I've heard that lady speak on a radio talk show recently," she said when I told her what we had seen on TV.

"Really? You know who I'm talking about then?" I asked excitedly.

"Yes. She made some kind of squeeze box or something."

"That's right. Well, after watching her and hearing what she had to say . . ." I was afraid to go on, thinking how drastic my next statement would sound. "We think Drew is autistic."

"You do?" came the careful reply.

"Yes. Of course I'm embarrassed to say it since we don't have an official diagnosis or anything," I admitted, ignoring my disappointment that her response was not what I'd expected.

"Well, the best thing to do would be to find out if what you suspect is true or not. For your own peace of mind you should just get him tested and see."

Her calm and confident manner, although a surprise, was a reassuring sign to me that we weren't just making it all up.

She went on, "If I were you, I would go to the library and see what I could read about it. That will help you to know, too."

With the initial blurting of the dreadful "A" word now behind me, I expected to share in some emotion with her. I knew that her steady words of advice were good, but what I really wanted to hear was a gasp of utter surprise: "No! How could you even think that! There's just no way that could possibly be true!"

As we continued to talk, I had an ever-so-slight feeling that she had perhaps imagined having this very conversation with me some day. No shock, no horror, no denial of the monster's existence in Drew. Her words were noticeably one beat delayed when she went to answer my next question, "Has anyone from church ever said anything to you about autism in connection with Drew?"

"Yes," finally came her soft but honest reply.

"They have?" I gasped with disbelief. "Who? Tell me who thought Drew was autistic." I pressed, not stopping to think of the difficult and very uncomfortable position in which I was putting my friend.

"Well," she continued very gently, and then proceeded to list three or four names of ladies from church, all of whom worked or had worked professionally with children at some point in time.

"You're kidding," I said more to myself than to her. The very idea of being the topic of conversation and never having a clue about it made me feel instantly embarrassed. Just like the emperor's new clothes— none could be seen, but everybody knew, everybody saw, and nobody said a word. At least not to me.

Here I had been, parading into church each week in just my underwear, and nobody had said a thing to me. How did everyone else know about autism and not us? We were the very ones that had been living with it from the beginning. We had eaten with it, slept with it, ridden in the car with it. It had played with Drew's toys, worn Drew's clothes—existed in my arms at birth! Yet on we went, our eyes blind to its reality. How foolish I felt.

"What about you? Did you think so too?" I had to know.

"I had some concerns," she continued to speak carefully. "Are you upset no one said anything?"

Thinking a moment of what it would be like to be in their shoes, I had to admit, "No. How can I be?" I knew I never would have had the guts to tell another mother that I thought something was wrong with her child. When you aren't asked, how can you tell? I saw the silence as an expression of love for me, not maliciousness. Perhaps I would have defensively laughed in their faces if anyone had made such a suggestion to me. The Lord was very gracious to us in how He let us know, saving us from potential hurt and bitterness toward the brethren. No, I was thankful no one had said anything. It was something we needed to learn for ourselves and in the Lord's timing.

After my conversation with Lorie Ann, my obsessive nature was revived, only this time with a vengeance. This was my son we were talking about. I was responsible for him and it was up to me to figure things out so that we could help him. The first thing that needed to be done was a mending of understanding between David and me. If we were to help Drew at all, it had to be together.

Sitting together that evening on the couch, talking about the now one main focus of our lives, David tenderly took my hands in his. Looking at him, with my now perpetually reddened eyes, I searched his face. How could we be divided from each other during a time of such hurt? We were each other's best friend. We needed each other. Not just for each other, but for Drew's sake.

"I just don't like to see you so sad all of the time," he said softly.

He did care! And he cared about me! "Oh, David," I cried, burying my face in his neck and sobbing all over again. "Why don't you feel this sadness with me?" I asked almost beggingly.

"It's not that I don't feel sad," he began, searching for the right words. "It's just that I don't show it like you do. When I see you just crying and lying on the couch I get frustrated because I want to fix things and I know I just can't," he ended.

I should have realized that David had a need, not just because he was a man but, more vitally, because it was his livelihood as a mechanic, to fix things, make them all work right. On the job he was challenged as he worked on cars to figure out the car's exact problem by listening to it and looking at the engine. What a feeling of worthiness and accomplishment he would rightly feel when a car he'd seen towed in and which he had worked on was able to be driven out. This wasn't a selfish pride but something put by God into the nature of man: to use your brain, to think, to calculate, to reason to a logical conclusion, and then to persevere to right what is wrong.

There is a natural sense of triumph that work and sweat bring to mankind, with the obvious fruit of the labors of his hands before him. It is a gift from God. From David's perspective, there was no clear direction to take, no leads to follow, no concrete numbers to calculate, and no tools in his hands with which to fix his broken son. He was lost. We were both lost, wandering in the dark trying to find our beloved boy whose lostness was worse than our own. I began to realize that not only did David have grief, his was perhaps greater, due to his sense of frustration and his inability to do what he had been created to do—fix. I felt guilty for accusing David of not caring for Drew. Tears were all I had, but I was united again with my husband. We were more entwined than I even knew. We prayed to God, pouring out our hearts as never before, to please help us. Please, please help us.

The Lord giveth, and the Lord taketh away. Blessed be the name of the Lord.

12

God Shall Alone the Refuge Be

Not knowing the official procedure to take when you suspect your son is autistic, I called my pediatrician the following day.

"Umm, David and I were watching TV a few nights ago," I told him, "and, umm, well, we saw this show about an autistic woman—and, umm, well . . ." There was silence on the other end of the receiver. "Well, we think Drew is autistic," I finally blurted.

What a fool he must take me for, I thought. Waiting for him to chuckle and tell me that my fears were unfounded, I was surprised by his ready response.

"The best thing to do is to obtain a diagnosis. I'll refer you to Mary Bridge Children's Hospital."

"Can't you just give us a diagnosis?" I asked.

"No. It really would be better to have some experts in this area take a look at him. The hospital is set up with what's called a multidisciplinary team of professionals who will each take a look at Drew, and Dr. Horton*, the pediatric developmentalist, will then give a diagnosis and a follow-up treatment plan."

I felt overwhelmed at the thought of a bunch of strangers observing Drew.

"So what do I do?" I asked, feeling a bit foolish for not knowing.

"Just call and set up an appointment with Dr. Horton" came the reply.

After hanging up the phone, I thought, *Now we are getting somewhere. The professionals will be able to help us out.*

I called the hospital that day to set up an appointment with Dr. Horton. I was amazed at the length of time we would have to wait

---

* Name has been changed to protect identity.

before we could actually get in to see him.

"Six weeks!" I exclaimed back at the nurse who took my call.

I had an overwhelming desire to get this diagnosis over with so that we could get on to helping Drew. I knew that because of our lack of knowledge of his problem we had already wasted valuable time.

"Well, if that's the soonest we can get in, go ahead and schedule it," I said, marking my calendar for six and a half weeks from that day's date.

Another appointment would have to be made to spend an entire day with the speech therapist, physical therapist, occupational therapist, social worker, and psychologist. I made the arrangements. They would be sending me the paperwork to fill out and return to them before my scheduled appointment with the doctor.

Meanwhile, I was on the rampage to figure out what autism was all about. I would return from the library with an armload of books to read. A friend with Internet access was able to obtain some information for me to read right away. As I read, I became consumed with grief. If our hunches were accurate, and we believed they were, a bleak future stared our autistic son in the face. The more I read, the deeper was my plunge into the pit of despair. Not only was I having to deal with my grief over Drew's condition, but I was the sole person on whom lay the responsibility of figuring out what to do about it. David had no time to sit and read the pile of information. It was up to me.

Driven by my compulsion to figure out what to do about it, I got on the phone and called anyone and everyone who would talk to me.

"Hello. My name is Cathy," I would say. "I understand you are a Christian mother with an autistic child."

My real interest was to contact someone who was like-minded in the areas of theology, education, and parenting. Somehow, I always managed to find, by word of mouth, a Christian mother. But not all were aligned with me in doctrine or education. For instance, one mother I talked to said, "Yes. Our Danny was diagnosed a year ago when he was three."

"What are you doing for him?" I questioned.

"Well, we believe he is healed."

Despite this declaration, she told me that they put him in a special preschool run by the state. And to top it off, I could hear screaming in the background.

"Thank you for your time," I managed to say before hanging up.

The next parent I called had an adolescent boy who was institutionalized. We were both Christian mothers with similar parenting philosophies.

"Don't you think that one's parenting philosophy affects the treatment?" I asked.

Her voice was curt as she told me, "Don't you know that ninety percent of couples who have an autistic child end up divorced?"

I recoiled, knowing my meager knowledge of autism. This was not an encouraging statistic.

"Thank you," I said before hanging up the receiver. What were we to do?

Despite the information I was receiving on the phone from other mothers and fathers, I was determined to find the best possible solution. I desperately wanted to hear a mother respond with, "Yes, my son has been cured from autism. All you have to do is ———."

I talked to strangers all over the United States. I would get their names and numbers from people who knew about them. "So-and-so knows so-and-so and she has an autistic child. She lives in California. Her number is ———." From as many people as I contacted, I got differing opinions, not only about the origin of the problem, but also about the preferred treatment method.

I continued my reading of materials from the library. No one could give me any real direction, so I just began with the list of books under "autism." Again, the more I read about this syndrome, the more confused I became. Some experts reported that the parents, namely the mother, had something to do with the acquisition of this devastating problem. Others said it happened in the womb. Others claimed it was genetic, while still others said it was a result of diet and allergic reactions. Despite my research, I was no closer to the answer. Not only could the experts not agree on the origin of the problem, a common agreement could not be reached for how to treat it.

My biggest concern was over the persons in the forefront of the "battle," leading the way toward understanding autism. Since it was a syndrome that could be diagnosed only by observing behavior, not an objective medical test, the almighty psychologists were the leading experts. As a Christian I had difficulty accepting one word a psychologist had to say about anything. I knew that the philosophy of modern-day psychology was, for the most part, antithetical to the worldview which I held as a Christian.

I quickly rejected the view that I had done this to my child. The "refrigerator mother," they called it. Because of my supposed lack of love and ability to bond with my child, he felt rejected and withdrew not only from my affection, but also from all of humanity. Elliot's loving nature quickly dismissed this notion. I was the same mother to both children—one child was responsive, and one was not. In fact, Drew's behavior demanded so much of me that if anybody was "neglected," it was Elliot. I clearly had nothing to do with Drew's distant and withdrawn behavior because I was the same loving mother to both children.

Looking for somebody to blame, I turned to David.

"I always said we would have a child with something wrong with him if you refused to wear a mask while doing brake work on a car," I accused him one day.

I had been to David's work place and had noticed the sign which read that all technicians were to wear protective masks while working around the fumes of a brake system. I had turned to David and asked, "You wear one, don't you?"

"Are you kidding? No one really does that."

Undoubtedly, his negligent behavior had contributed to Drew's dilemma.

I began to go nuts trying to think of a reason to pin Drew's autism on. Deep down I didn't really believe it was David. Maybe it was the aspirin I took when I was pregnant . . . maybe it was the hot tub I sat in when I didn't realize I was even pregnant . . . maybe, maybe, maybe. Who could tell? There were no answers.

There was just as much confusion surrounding what should be done for the autistic child. The myriad therapies were mind-boggling. How was I supposed to figure out which was best? I already felt that time was against us since we found out so late in his life that something was wrong with him. I felt like Atlas, with the entire world slung over my shoulder. What a burden. How was I to bear it?

Not long after our discovery of Drew's problem we happened to sing a certain hymn at church. For many months the words of this hymn would be my sole comfort and encouragement.

> God shall alone the refuge be,
>   And comfort of my mind;
> Too wise to be mistaken, He,
>   Too good to be unkind.
>
> In all his holy, sovereign will,
>   He is, I daily find,
> Too wise to be mistaken, still
>   Too good to be unkind.
>
> When I the tempter's rage endure,
>   'Tis God supports my mind;
> Too wise to be mistaken, sure,
>   Too good to be unkind.

When sore afflictions on me lie,
    He is (though I am blind)
Too wise to be mistaken, yea,
    Too good to be unkind.

What though I can't his goings see,
    Nor all his footsteps find?
Too wise to be mistaken, He,
    Too good to be unkind.

Hereafter he will make me know,
    And I shall surely find,
He was too wise to err, and O,
    Too good to be unkind.

(By Samuel Medley, from A *Selection of Hymns for Public Worship* by William Gadsby)

The paperwork from the hospital arrived within a few days. I ripped open the envelope and shuffled through the pile of papers it contained.

"Mary Bridge Children's Hospital and Health Center—Neuro-development Program Parent Questionnaire," it was titled.

The number of questions and the type of information they wanted were intimidating: questions about the child's birth, family history, pregnancy history, newborn history, history of his general health, feed-ing/communication, and, finally, temperament and behavior. I then found a child-monitoring questionnaire that needed to be filled out as well. That packet had specific directions for having your child perform certain activities in the following areas:

- Communication
- Gross motor skills
- Fine motor skills

- Adaptive skills
- Personal/social

"Whew!" I said to David when he came home from work that evening. "Can you believe all of these questions?"

David began reading through some of the material and could tell, right away, that Drew was unable to perform many of the activities. We both agreed that filling out all of the preliminary paperwork was going to be a job all its own.

The thing that continued to nag me was the fact we had to subject Drew—and ourselves for that matter—to the scrutiny of a psychologist. I never thought I would ever find myself in a situation like this. The view a psychologist had of a child and his nature would be very different from the view David and I held, due to our understanding of the Scriptures, specifically, that a child by nature is a direct descendant of Adam, and therefore a fallen creature unable to love God and follow His commandments. The causes of Drew's behavior could easily be misconstrued due to the psychologist's gross misunderstanding of a child's nature. It would only follow that the treatment plan suggested would be faulty as well.

We still had six weeks before our first appointment. I would try to learn all that I could. Perhaps there was another way.

13
Whate'er My God Ordains Is Right

The only difference in our home life was a simple change of perspective. Drew was the same crying child he had always been. But now I saw him in a different light. His cries had real concrete meaning, meaning only Drew knew. They meant more than just rebellion against my authority—they were bigger, much bigger. Despite the new-found knowledge of the fact that something was wrong with him, I still tried to continue treating him the same way, holding him to the same standard of self-control—only now with more patience and understanding. The question now was: "How do I know what behaviors are due to his autism and what behaviors are simply pure rebellion?" All we could think to do was to learn everything we could about this syndrome so that we could accommodate Drew's frame to the best of our abilities and establish a standard we could hold him to as we had always done.

My sister, Chris, had been talking to some people from her church and autism came up. Someone knew a Christian mother who home-schooled her children and lived right here in town. Chris called me with the phone number one day.

I had such a yearning to see another child like Drew. I had so many questions. Maybe there was really nothing wrong with Drew after all. Seeing this other child would help me know.

After hanging up with my sister, I dialed the number on my piece of paper. The phone rang on the other line.

"Hello," said a harried voice after several rings.

"Hi. My name is Cathy and your number was given to me by someone who knows you. I understand you have an autistic son and I was wondering if we could meet. I would really like to talk to you."

"Oh, do you have an autistic, too?" She sounded almost excited.

"Well, yes—at least I think I do. We haven't gotten an official diagnosis yet, but I'm pretty sure based on everything I know." I stumbled over my words to answer her question. I was still not used to the sound of it. "I have an autistic child . . . ." The words ran through my head.

"Sure. C'mon over," she replied and we set up a time before hanging up.

I couldn't wait to meet her. Maybe she could help me figure out how to help Drew.

On the following Monday morning David drove me to meet the mother with the autistic boy. I was nervous as we pulled up in front of the huge two-story house.

"I shouldn't be long," I told David as I got out of the car.

Drew began to cry as I got out, but the usual sound of terror and panic was silenced when I closed the door of the car. I couldn't subject this kind woman to my son's unpredictable cries and screams. Drew would stay with brother and Daddy so that I could talk and absorb whatever lay before me without distraction.

A short, dark-haired woman opened the door before I even reached the front porch. The faces of three inquisitive children emerged from behind her. *Which one is it?* I wondered, climbing the front steps.

"Hi. Are you Cathy?" came her friendly voice.

"Yes," I answered, smiling.

"Well I'm Kris* and this is my Trey*," she said, touching the head of a perfectly normal looking five-year-old boy.

"Hi, Trey," I said gently, careful not to make any sudden moves toward him.

I wanted time to stand still so that I could stare at this little boy, watch his every move, listen to his voice. I wanted to see if I could see Drew in him. Was there anything that looked familiar? A part of me was hoping there wouldn't be. There was still a possibility that we had

* Names have been changed to protect identity.

92

made all of this up in our heads. We had no diagnosis—nothing to prove anything about Drew. Perhaps I was just wasting this poor woman's time.

As I locked eyes with Trey, however, I saw it. Despite my efforts to be non-intrusive, a look was all he could take. Immediately his eyes shifted away with an all-too-familiar faraway look. He ran screaming into another room.

Kris appeared unfazed and proceeded to introduce me to her other two older children.

"C'mon in," she motioned to me.

The living room was sparsely but tastefully furnished. The two older children began to occupy themselves with quiet activities in an adjoining room. As I sat down, I noticed a pile of papers and books on the floor next to the couch. Kris picked them up and began to go through them, saying I could borrow them for as long as I needed. These materials were what she had found most helpful.

Trey entered the room looking sideways in my direction. It was clear he found my presence there disconcerting. As I listened to Kris talk, my eyes would drift to Trey. I caught him several times staring clearly at me with a look of curiosity; but as soon as eye contact was made, he would look away and scream.

"No!" yelled Kris. "No screaming!"

Trey plopped to the floor and began playing with a pile of marbles, crashing them one at a time into a plastic urn.

It was hard to concentrate or to even finish a thought with Kris because of the intermittent screaming, punctuated constantly by "No! No!"

Kris told me she was a Christian and that she also enjoyed home-schooling her children. Just the combination I was looking for. She handed me a book called *Let me Hear Your Voice*, by Catherine Maurice, and another entitled *The Me Book*, by Ivar Lovaas.

"This is what we use with Trey. Behavior Modification," Kris said.

Trey let out another shrill screech, his head flying back as he let it out. Even though this had happened numerous times already during my short visit, I still jumped.

"No screaming," his mother bellowed at almost the same intensity as the scream.

Trey echoed, "No screaming," in a soft voice to himself. Picking up a handful of marbles, he held them oddly to the corner of his eyes before throwing them all at the urn. I started to feel a little nauseated. And to think I was worried about Drew bothering her with his cries. *How does she manage with all of this noise?* I wondered.

As we talked, I learned that Trey had been subjected to a home program of behavior modification and then, because it was believed to help even more, he was enrolled in the public school's special needs preschool. He was starting his third year with the school system. I tried to imagine how much worse he must have been before he had received all of this professional help. It was clear that life with Trey was difficult. Thankfully, the other two children were quiet; I almost forgot that they were there.

Besides the materials she lent me, the best information I received that day was that we could get a diagnosis from a pediatric neurologist—it wasn't necessary to involve a psychologist. She hadn't.

After saying good-bye and climbing back into the car, I thanked David for being so patient. He had given the boys some snacks we had packed. The atmosphere was calm and quiet as little mouths in the backseat finished up their fruit bars.

"Oh, David," I moaned, "we have it so good."

I turned around to look at Drew. His blue eyes were clear but distant as he sat mesmerized by the world passing outside his window as David drove us home.

With crumbs around his little mouth, he looked so helpless and dependent. I reached to brush the crumbs from his lips, but he jerked away from my hand. He showed no sign of happiness to have me back in the car where I belonged. All of his shrieks and tears when I had gotten out of the car earlier were nothing more than a desire for sameness. In his mind I should not have left my spot in the front seat—nothing more. His screams were no different from the screams that rang from Trey's mouth when I entered his home. I didn't belong there—I should not be there. The order of life had been messed up. As I could not take Trey's screams at me as personal, neither could I take Drew's cries as personal. It was the latter realization that pierced me.

I was too emotionally drained to relate my visit to David. Even though he was very interested, he could see I just couldn't talk right then. This was just the beginning of our search for help for our son. It remained an uphill climb.

The day after my visit with Kris, I called my pediatrician and asked him if it was really necessary to get a diagnosis. We were still skeptical of having to go through the process of getting one by subjecting Drew and ourselves to a psychologist. By now, after the reading I had done, we found Drew to fit perfectly into the profile of autism; why should we pay a bunch of money to have someone with some letters after their name tell it to our faces? But the doctor said that he thought it best—if for no other reason than to eliminate the possibility of it being anything else.

"Plus," he added, "the diagnostic team at Mary Bridge Hospital would be able to evaluate Drew and determine for sure if he is developing and functioning according to his age."

"Well, since autism isn't a psychological problem but rather a neurological one, could we get the diagnosis from a pediatric neurologist instead?" I asked, trying to sound as well-informed as possible.

He sounded hesitant. "The thing about having a diagnostic team look at him is that it will give us a clear picture of where he's at. Really, they are the best in this area." He seemed perplexed.

"What if we got the actual diagnosis from the neurologist and the developmental profile through Child Find, with the school district?"

Kris had told me about this wonderful testing procedure the school district offered for free. (Supposedly free—paid for in full by our tax dollars.) If we went through Mary Bridge, we would have to pay nearly five hundred dollars out of our pocket because our insurance did not cover this type of evaluation, even if referred by our physician—which it had been. David and I reasoned that by using a pediatric neurologist and the Child Find team, we would be accomplishing the same thing, only we would be spending less money and would not need to deal with a psychological evaluation.

My pediatrician agreed but still sounded confused as to why we would pass up the best diagnostic team in the whole Pacific Northwest.

So it was settled. I called Mary Bridge and canceled our appointment, then called and made an appointment with the most well thought-of pediatric neurologist in the area, Dr. Carl Franken*. Next I called the school district and was told when the next evaluation day was scheduled and when to take Drew in. I would be receiving some sort of confirmation in the mail soon. All of this done, it was now time to wait.

It was up to me to do the research. So I did. I read and read every day. I continued to call faceless strangers that I found out about by word of mouth. With each book I read and each person I talked to I came away with a new gem of wisdom. Sometimes it was a very tiny gem, but a gem just the same. Oftentimes I gleaned a powerful lesson in what *not* to do with my child.

Every night I dumped on David everything I was learning. He would listen with interest. He was my sounding board, and we never needed each other more. Sometimes we talked late into the night thinking we were actually beginning to see through this impossible darkness. Those were the hopeful nights as we fell asleep together, holding on to each

* Name has been changed to protect identity.

other, thankful we were not traversing this road alone, and thanking God for His goodness to us because our lives could have been much, much worse.

Of course the doubtful times would creep back to haunt us, and there were the horrible days when we felt as if we had only come full circle and hadn't really learned anything at all.

Drew's personality continued to be distant, hollow, forever crying, forever sad, forever unreachable. By the time I dropped into bed each night, I was exhausted from dealing with Drew all day. In addition, because of my tired state of mind, I was unable to see any light at the end of the tunnel. Nothing ahead but blackness. Despite my frantic and aimless pursuits to help our lost son, I was finding myself lost, too. Deeper and darker I plunged into confusion and grief. There just were no easy answers, no quick fix to remedy the daunting future which lay before us.

One beautiful June Sunday I had a difficult time at church, looking into the eyes of all of the mothers who had suspected autism in Drew. I glanced down with embarrassment after a quick "Good morning."

Only Lorie Ann knew our thoughts and I had asked her to keep them quiet until we knew for sure.

That evening a social event was held at the home of one of our friends. The entire church had been invited. I was nervous when we arrived, as I always was whenever we went anywhere out of the ordinary with Drew. When we entered, the place was packed with people chattering in small groups and eating. It was difficult to move around. One of us always held tightly to Drew's hand. You never knew what he might do. Despite the chaos of the laughing crowd, however, Drew, stiff with nerves himself, managed to get through the group. He usually did fine until someone trapped him with a social pleasantry such as "Hello, Drew." Most people, however, had already learned their lesson with Drew and just gave him a noncommittal smile.

Gradually, the relaxed mood rubbed off on me and soon David and I were enjoying separate conversations with other people. It felt good to be with the brethren, talking about something other than autism. I found myself chatting with a woman I didn't know very well. She and her husband and two small children had been attending for only a short time. It was wonderful to get to know her and to discuss the things of the Lord.

I could see Drew out of the corner of my eye, lost in his own world despite the sea of humanity surrounding him. He had found the door out to the patio and was opening and closing it, over and over again. He stopped periodically to jiggle the doorknob. Even though this repetitive, non-productive activity seemed odd (none of the other children in attendance were lined up to play with the door), I was glad Drew was "happy" and busy so that I had a chance to mingle.

After over an hour and a half had passed and some people had already gone home, I noticed Drew still at it with the door. *Open, close, open, close, open, close, jiggle, jiggle, jiggle* . . . . His behavior seemed more noticeable now that the room had cleared out somewhat. Still sensitive about the quiet conversations about Drew among some of the women, I impulsively blurted out that we thought Drew might be autistic. I thought that this bold and confident declaration might show we weren't as ignorant as everyone thought. I guessed as well that everyone must be thinking it anyway as they could easily spy Drew's obsessive behavior with the door.

"Really?" came one mother's response as she turned to look at Drew. She seemed sincerely surprised. "He looks fine to me," she continued.

Now I wished I hadn't said anything. Why did I have to bring it up?

"What is autism anyway?" she turned back to me and asked.

I tripped over my words trying to describe autism to her. Just how do you answer a question like that? It was as if I had just been asked to give a quick, pat answer to an unanswerable question.

I fumbled with some characteristics I could remember from the reading I had done.

"Well, autistics don't understand abstracts so they don't follow humor," I stated with confidence, knowing this to be true as I had just read something about it the day before.

"Mmm. My daughter doesn't get jokes either," she chuckled to herself. "Maybe she's autistic, too."

"No! You don't get what I'm saying!" I wanted to yell at her. "It's bigger than just not getting the punch line of a joke!"

I saw that it was best to just remain quiet about it. I was suddenly very tired and went to find David so that we could go home. How could I explain this horrible monster to that lady or to anyone? I didn't even understand it myself.

My plunge into the pit of despair picked up momentum with every book and article I read. "Hopeless," "permanent," "lifelong" were the words that seemed to be popping up everywhere I looked. Despite all of the talk of "improvement" with this therapy and "increased function" with that therapy, the word I was frantically searching for was nowhere to be found: "cured." With knowledge came mourning. Even with my growing understanding of this confusing menace, no comfort or solace came with it. Only numbing fear and a silent terror. Again, there was only one place I could ever find real comfort or solace—not in anything I read in an article or scientific journal, but in the only place true peace was ever found: in the sovereignty of the living God.

One hymnwriter says it best:

> Whate'er my God ordains is right:
> Holy his will abideth;
> I will be still whate'er he doth,
> And follow where he guideth:
> He is my God;
> Though dark my road,
> He holds me that I shall not fall:
> Wherefore to him I leave it all.

Whate'er my God ordains is right
He never will deceive me;
He leads me by the proper path;
I know he will not leave me
I take, content, what he hath sent;
His hand can turn my griefs away,
And patiently I wait his day.

Whate'er my God ordains is right:
Though now this cup, in drinking,
May bitter seem to my faint heart,
I take it, all unshrinking:
My God is true,
Each morn anew
Sweet comfort yet shall fill my heart,
And pain and sorrow shall depart.

Whate'er my God ordains is right:
Here shall my stand be taken;
Though sorrow, need, or death be mine,
Yet am I not forsaken;
My Father's care
Is round me there;
He holds me that I shall not fall
And so to him I leave it all.

(Words by Samuel Rodigast, translated by Catherine Winkworth)

The following day was a bit cool but sunny and crystal clear. I felt as
though we had been locked in an unreal world for a year. We needed a
distraction, some happiness. We decided to take the children to the
park. The sunshine lifted my spirits and the children's faces filled my

heart with love. For the moment we were as we had been before, before the knowledge of the dreadful monster. Drew seemed calm and cooperative as we dressed him for the park. Easygoing Elliot gave me his shiniest smile while I put his tiny shoes on his feet. All seemed right with the world. Just a normal family going to the park for the afternoon. David found a parking place near the tot lot and we all piled out. David took Drew's hand. "C'mon, Drew!"

I watched them run off toward the playground equipment. David seemed happy to be out with the boys, and I smiled to myself to see his relaxed face. Carrying Elliot, I found an empty toddler swing and buckled him in. The sun felt warm on my hair and the giggles coming from Elliot caused me to instantly relax.

"Is this fun?" I asked the back of Elliot's hood. His continuing noises of glee assured me he thought it was.

I scanned the play area and saw the usual scene: a small group of mothers talking and laughing over at the picnic table and a few preschool-aged children running free and wild over the playground equipment. As I was searching for a sight of David and Drew, I was snapped back to reality by the sound of Drew's very distinctive, very loud voice.

"Ohhh noooo! Did you want to do that?" (Translated: "I want to do that.")

Everyone around him couldn't help but hear the now-incessant pronoun reversal (substituting "you" for "I") which peppered his language. *Why don't you just wear a sign that reads, "I'm autistic"?* I thought to myself with embarrassment. I lowered my eyes and concentrated on the moving shadow of the swing under Elliot and his relaxed and happy demeanor.

Drew's voice continued to bellow across the space between us, but my discomfort dissipated as I realized that no one else was really paying attention. I was ashamed of my feelings of embarrassment over Drew. The euphoria from the sunny day was now overshadowed by the reminder of the monster's presence with us. How could I pretend to ignore it? It was always going to be with us . . . no matter where we went.

❖ ❖ ❖

The day arrived, at the end of July, for David and me to take Drew in for his evaluation with the school district. Drew was three years and eleven months old; he would turn four the following month. Even though I had an anxious anticipation to hear the truth, I was a knot of tangled nerves. Not having slept much the night before, I rose early to get the children ready. Not only was it a stressful day because of Drew, but it was the first time I had ever left Elliot with a sitter. Jayni, our pastor's wife, had agreed to take him for the entire morning. Although I trusted her completely, I wanted to cry when I handed her my sweet baby.

"Don't worry," she soothed. "We'll be just fine. Take your time. I have all kinds of fun planned for us," she said, nestling Elliot against her.

On the drive over to the school building, I turned around to look at Drew. He had no clue what this day held for him. He just rode along in the car and went wherever it took him. He seemed so little and helpless, riding all alone in the big back seat. He was alone, all right. Locked in a world all his own, unpenetrable, amputated from the rest of us. I felt a desperate need to hold him and love him.

"I love you, sweetie," I choked out to him.

No response. Not even a flicker of recognition that I was speaking to him. I turned around and fought the tears. Now was not the time to cry. We had a long day ahead.

We parked the car and slowly got out. I peered up at the old, crumbling building before us and shivered despite the incredible heat of the day. I had the feeling of one about to take the most important test of his life. Pass or fail: Which would it be?

Each of us holding one of Drew's hands, we entered the building and were greeted cordially by Dan Campbell*, the man in charge of Child Find.

---

* Name has been changed to protect identity.

"And this must be Drew," he stated in a distracted tone as he flipped through some papers.

We were given some forms and a name tag to stick on Drew.

"Nooo thank youuu," came Drew's shrill voice as he whipped his name off his shirt.

"He's never liked sticky things touching him," I offered to the room full of people.

"That's okay," Mr. Campbell said, still appearing distracted by paperwork. "Just follow me. You'll be seeing the physical therapist first to assess Drew's gross motor skills*."

We were led into an upstairs room filled with various pieces of equipment. The physical therapist seemed just as distracted with her paperwork but glanced up for an instant to say hello.

She had Drew walk up and down some stairs. He was unable to alternate his feet each step and still descended the stairs as a toddler would.

At home he was unable to pedal his tricycle, but here he managed to pedal the therapy bike a few feet across the carpeting.

"Hurray," I cheered Drew on.

Feeling a little silly for being the only one in the room rejoicing in Drew's triumph, I shut up. I forgot this was a test, an evaluation, not a game. This was serious. Drew was then asked to do some balancing, jumping, hopping on one foot, and throwing and catching a bouncing ball. After a brief pause, the therapist announced her assessment that Drew was only slightly delayed in his gross motor skills—nothing that would need professional therapy.

"Whew," I smiled at David, beginning to feel more confident.

We were then ushered into another room to have the occupational therapist work with Drew. Instantly, I didn't like her. The room seemed cramped and disorganized. With the sweltering heat that day, I felt

* Gross motor: The use of large muscle groups that coordinate body movements required for normal living, such as walking, running, jumping, throwing, and balance.

suffocated in the small room. A fan was blasting in one corner, flipping some papers stacked near it. The hum of the fan seemed to be in competition with the small radio playing near it. I was no expert in autism, but I thought at least the professionals would know better than to test an autistic child in the midst of such sensory chaos. The large-framed woman scooted a small chair near the short table where she was seated and motioned to us to seat Drew next to her. David and I felt like intruders as we observed, standing behind them. Without even greeting Drew or David and me, she dumped some popcorn kernels on the table and gave Drew a small bottle with a narrow opening.

"Put the kernels into the bottle, one at a time. Go as fast as you can," she said, as if reading directions off a label. She set her stop watch and blurted, "Go!"

Drew seemed a bit baffled about what was expected out of him while he fingered the clear bottle in his hands.

"Put these into the bottle, honey," I said slowly while pointing to the items on the table.

The therapist threw me a look that plainly said, "Butt out."

After being silenced by the corporal, I started to perspire. My stomach and neck were tense with anticipation. "Keep going—you can do it," I softly cheered to Drew as he managed to put the kernels into the bottle, ignoring my earlier rebuke to not interfere.

I wanted Drew to win, to pass the test with flying colors. I felt he deserved a medal for not crying once and for participating so well up until now. So many strangers. So many new sounds and sensations. A new chair to sit in. A new building to be in. New smells to take in. So much heat. So much demand placed on my little afflicted one. I was proud of him as he followed these stranger's commands and tried to do what he was told. I wanted them to appreciate all that was good about him . . . there was so much good about him. It seemed nobody was interested in what he could do and in his amazing abilities. I wanted them to ask him to read and count. No. They only seemed to want to know what he couldn't do and where he was "below." That's all anyone saw or looked for.

The therapist continued to have Drew try using some scissors and drawing a circle on a piece of paper. After only a few minutes, she had her expert assessment.

"He seems to be just slightly below average with fine motor abilities. Nothing to worry about though. Just try and practice with some scissors at home."

That's it? I thought. *Just have him practice with some scissors at home?* I was beginning to feel that all of this anxiety was for nothing. There's nothing wrong with Drew. We could cut to his heart's content with some scissors at home. No problem.

With more uplifted spirits, we walked Drew to see the next professional down the hall. The speech therapist was warm and talkative. Her red hair and freckles defined a kind face. She found chairs for all of us and then sat across from Drew at a small desk. Drew was becoming a bit bored by now with all of the testing. He was restless and fidgety in his tiny chair. I was dripping wet from nerves and the heat.

C'mon, honey, I thought, *keep going. You're doing great. Let's just get through this.*

The speech therapist was animated and friendly. She spoke to David and me as if we were fellow humans, and she treated Drew professionally. She had a fast pace as she flipped through her spiral notebook and asked Drew to point to different pictures.

"Great!" "Wow!" "Good job!" were frequent encouragements she showered on Drew. I was actually beginning to relax a little. This wasn't going to be so bad.

"What is this?" asked the therapist as she pointed to a picture.

"Carousel," answered Drew.

The therapist stopped short, her mouth gaping wide. "No one has ever gotten that one before," she gasped in disbelief. "If I ever do get an answer," she continued, "it's a merry-go-round. Carousel is actually the accurate answer."

I wanted to kiss this lady for seeing Drew as a person and actually taking joy in his accomplishments. David tossed me a wink as he took my sweaty hand in his.

"Well," she said as she finished up with Drew, "you can really see that he has been worked with at home."

David squeezed my hand. *Yes, he has—quite a bit, as a matter of fact—and thank you for noticing,* I thought to myself.

We were to go on ahead with a special education instructor in another room while the speech therapist tallied up Drew's scores. By now an hour had passed and even I was ready to be done. Certainly Drew was more than ready as well. The heat was becoming unbearable the closer to noon it got. The old building was like an oven. I could tell that Drew had gone as far as he could and I was waiting for some kind of eruption. Who knew which demand would cause it to happen?

Drew was to be tested on pre-academic skills.

"He is really going to blow them out of the water on this one," I smiled to myself, thinking of Drew's amazing abilities with letters and numbers.

We followed a special education teacher to a room in the back of the building where a small table and chairs for all of us were placed near an open window. We all took our seats. The teacher was stiff and distant. She had much the same heavy persona we had encountered earlier with some of the others. She sat opposite Drew behind the little table. A large box of items sat on the floor near her chair. She laid out different lengths of straws. Drew began to play with them.

"No. Keep them right here on the table, please," she said, removing a straw from Drew's grasp. "Tell me which straw is the longest," she asked slowly.

No answer.

She repeated her question in the same robotic fashion, "Which straw is the longest?"

Again, no answer.

"Which straw is the shortest?" she continued with her line of questioning.

Drew's attention had been drawn to the straws long enough. "Do you want me to pick them up?" he seemed to ask as he began to play with the pile in front of him.

"Okay. All done," she said, taking her property back.

I began to get nervous again. The stagnant air in the room weighed me down. I shot a panicky look in David's direction and couldn't help but notice the pained look on his face.

A similar line of questioning continued for what seemed like hours. More and more items were removed from her box and placed before Drew. More questions were asked, which quickly dissipated in the thickness of the room. Drew was clearly tired and distracted.

"You're doing a good job, sweetie. Good sitting." I tried to keep my voice from cracking.

She placed a small board in front of Drew and told him to reach around it and feel an item, such as a comb or toothbrush. She wanted him to identify the item without being able to see it. I felt sick when Drew simply picked up the board and began to play with it, turning it over in his hands.

Once again, so matter-of-factly, she removed her belongings from Drew's possession and placed them back in the box.

I started to squirm myself. It was as if Drew was on the witness stand, being interrogated by the prosecution. "Which one is soft?" "Which one is hard?" "What do we use to brush our hair?" "Why do we put things in the refrigerator?" "What can you use to roll?" "Which is heavier?"

Stop! Stop! Stop! I wanted to scream at the prosecution. *You're right! He's guilty! He's guilty! Are you finally happy you proved it? Just stop— please just stop!*

After what seemed an eternity, the questioning finally ended. The courtroom was silent except for the winning side, shuffling her precious evidence back into its box for the next unsuspecting defendant. Not one question about the alphabet. Not one question about whether he knew any numbers. If there had been, we would not have been on the losing side feeling this enormous weight of grief.

The last and final episode before we were released for the day was an interview with the school psychologist. Her position was not to give a diagnosis, only to see if he qualified to receive special educational services from the state.

We were greeted by a woman who looked exactly as I suspected she might: round with a blunt haircut and glasses—no makeup—gentle with an all-wise look in her eyes. I wondered what she was thinking as she looked us up and down.

"Please be seated." She politely motioned to two chairs opposite her at a large table.

"Do you want Drew to sit here, too?"

"No. Just let him play. I can observe him while we talk," she smiled. She proceeded to question us about Drew's ability to toilet himself, dress himself, and feed himself. She was really very nice and I quickly relaxed with her. She listened intently to our answers and at certain points would look startled and let out an "Aha!" and then scribble some notes on her paper. We obviously were saying the right things to spark her interest. We had no idea what she was searching for with her questions, but we tried to answer as accurately as possible.

When she seemed about through, she stopped to look at Drew with what appeared to be sincere interest. Without removing her eyes from him, she said, almost to herself, "He is certainly very well behaved. I know several teachers who would love to have him in their class."

David and I hadn't mentioned that we had no intention of using the school system for Drew's therapy but that we were simply interested in receiving an assessment from them. We just wanted to see how well Drew was functioning.

Before getting up to leave, I couldn't help but ask, "I realize you don't give a diagnosis, but could you tell me your opinion?" *Here I go.* "With all of this information you now have, would you consider Drew to be autistic?

Without missing a beat she nodded her head. "Yes."

She didn't realize that this was the first expert opinion we had heard. I felt as though someone had just kicked me in the stomach. I began to tremble. David took my hand under the table. Hot tears gathered in my eyes, blurring the psychologist's face. I turned to look at Drew. He was quietly absorbed with placing the letters of the alphabet in a neat, perfect row on the table. Defeat and pity consumed me.

Don't cry. Not in front of these uncaring, clinical professionals, I scolded myself.

The psychologist didn't even notice the emotional trauma she had just ignited.

There was a rustling of papers and some of the other therapists we had already seen that day entered the room. They seemed like characters from the far-off past. They congregated together and compared notes, thinking it ironic how some of them had come up with similar scores. They smiled and laughed with one another.

This is my child you are discussing! I wanted to scream and put an end to the lightheartedness. *This may just be your job, but this is my precious boy's future you are so flippantly talking about.*

With all of the self-control I could muster, I rose to discuss their findings.

The speech therapist spoke first. "It appears that Drew is functioning at about a two-and-a-half-year-old level." The lilt and bounce of her voice made me think she mistakenly thought she was sharing her favorite recipe with me.

Continuing to quiver uncontrollably and forcing the flood of tears back as hard as I could, I thanked everyone for their time.

We left, driving in silence to pick up Elliot. Drew nearly fell asleep on the short drive over. My heart ached for my Elliot. I almost couldn't wait to see him and hold him. I wanted to snuggle my perfect and healthy son.

"Please hurry, honey," I whispered to David.

"I know, love," he said as he reached to squeeze my limp hand in his. I closed my eyes and imagined Elliot's laughing eyes and longings to relate to us. My arms ached painfully for him—my sweet boy who could give me back the love I was feeling for his precious life. I needed the comfort that his little breathing body against mine would give.

We pulled into the driveway of Jayni's house. I couldn't get out of the car fast enough. We all waited at the door for only an instant after knocking. A smiling Jayni, holding a contented Elliot, greeted us with laughs and hellos. I grabbed Elliot and squeezed him to myself.

"Mommy missed you so much, sweetie," I said, soaking up the feeling of his warm, dewy face against mine. It was as if we had been away on a long and painful journey, but now we were back and reuniting ourselves again. Elliot leaned into me and I treasured his closeness. It lasted only a moment because he spotted his Daddy over my shoulder. His body wiggled with delight as he reached his tiny arms out for David. I handed Elliot over to David and we ascended the stairs into the living room. There were toys all over the place—remnants that told of a busy, fun experience. Drew shot past all of us and gravitated to the mini blinds by the sliding door windows. He ran his fingers over them and watched them sway back and forth in the sunlight.

"So how did everything go?" asked Jayni with interest, waiting expectantly to hear all of the details.

"Drew did fine," I began, watching the back of Drew's cocked head. The swinging blinds still interested him. He appeared as he truly was: odd and indifferent. The moving blinds seemed to be laughing at him as they danced before his eyes.

Unable to look Jayni in the eyes, I answered slowly and carefully, forming the painful words for the first time. I said, "They told us he is functioning at the level of a two-and-a-half-year-old." It finally happened. There was no more strength to hold it back. The dam broke loose. As fast as the torrent filled my eyes with tears, Jayni's arms were around me. I covered my face with my hands and shook with aching, silent sobs.

Embarrassed over my display of emotion and feeling a lack of stability, I pulled away and began picking up toys around my feet, not daring to look anyone in the face. I couldn't bear to read any pain or sympathy in Jayni's eyes. My own grief was already unmanageable.

The room was silent except for the tapping of the blinds against the window. I was anxious to get home, anxious to be private and sort out my thoughts. I desperately wanted to hold Drew and love him with a mother's comforting affection, soothe him and caress his weary face, so full of anxiety and confusion. I knew it was impossible to attempt such actions without the resulting screaming cry and desperate flight of escape. So I turned to Elliot when we got home and lavished him with my love and tenderness.

"My boy. My precious little boy," I whispered, rocking Elliot in my tired arms. Elliot heard me and grinned . . . even though my words were meant for another.

14
He Leads Me By the Proper Path

Drew turned four years old in August, the month following his barrage of tests. I maintained a routine of activities for Drew every day; reading picture books to him remained the biggest activity throughout the day. We would work on puzzles together or color with crayons. The routine benefited both Drew and me, brought some definition to our life, and helped us reach goals, mostly that of teaching Drew to take direction from me.

The area in which we worked with Drew the most continued to be that of his character. This had been the focus since we brought him home from the hospital the day he was born. Even the point of putting him on a feeding routine was to influence his character. We wanted to use the most commonplace of his daily activities—eating and sleeping— to teach him. By ordering his life for him, he learned from the start that he could count on us to meet his needs. He was the child, with foolishness in his sinful heart. We were responsible to train him to be patient, self-controlled, and respectful. We reminded ourselves of his natural tendency to lead, demand, control, and manipulate for his own wants. Our goal was to bring him from foolishness and self-centeredness to maturity and an ability to look beyond himself toward others. This was the message we tried to send Drew in all of our actions towards him. If it didn't begin at day one, when would it?

The principles found in Scripture which helped us define our views of our children's existence continued to guide and direct us in how we dealt with Drew. Just because we had been made aware of something horribly wrong with his brain did not change the fact that the condition of his heart was the same as it ever had been—lost and depraved. Being autistic did not mean that Drew was not a moral creature with a need for moral training. The moral training was just as important now as it had ever been.

Drew had learned already, to some degree, some of these Biblical character traits:

- Patience
- Self-control over his emotions, calming himself when upset
- Order (not for the need for sameness but rather learning to be helpful when asked to pick up toys, etc.)
- Self-control in learning to maintain his attention to an activity or task
- Following direction and being submissive when told to do something by an adult
- Being polite and respectful when someone greets him (showing consideration for others even though he couldn't say hi in response. He was made to shake hands if someone greeted him and not permitted to scream and pull away.)
- Gentleness (he was not allowed to be rough with animals or property despite feelings of frustration)
- Becoming accustomed to boundaries or limits placed on him

Our goal was to always consider Drew's character, and even though we were as consistent as possible and even at times weary over the apparent lack of improvement, we never forgot our responsibility to train and mold his conscience. That remained our highest duty to the children God had blessed us with. Scripture doesn't lower its standards of how man ought to behave, nor does it exempt one who is autistic . . . or has Attention Deficit Disorder, or Down's syndrome, or any other disorder. God's standards, like Himself, never change. It may be more difficult for some to reach certain standards than it is for others, but the standards remain. Our love for Drew didn't decrease when we learned of his disability. And how does a parent prove his love most to his child? By obeying the Lord who put the children in our care; viewing the child the way the Scriptures tell us to and not as the professional parenting experts of our day would like; being more concerned about his heart—not his supposedly fragile psyche. It was a far more loving act to demand that Drew get control over his exploding spirit than to allow him to spew forth whatever he felt, whenever he felt like it, and despite the reason for it. We could help Drew learn to control himself so that he wouldn't be controlled by his emotions. This conveyed more love than any embrace or kiss ever would. It would be a treasure he could carry with him throughout the rest of his life.

We continued with the same training we had always used. Our commands were given in a simple, clear manner, directly to his face. If disobeyed, we would either just put his body through the motions, or, if we could tell it was clearly defiance, he would be corrected immediately and at every offense. This could mean a flick to the lips for a mouth offense, a flick to the hand for touching something off limits, or discipline for obvious rebellion or a bad attitude. If he obeyed, praise and encouragement always followed . . . always. We used tangible rewards only when trying to teach a skill—like potty training—otherwise, it was mainly verbal praise. Drew acted as though physical affection was more punishment than anything else, so we just stuck to positive, happy-sounding words of encouragement. It was clear to us that consistency of approach was vital. Same reaction to the same offense, immediately, every time. The toll this effort took on me was overwhelming, but we tried to stay steady.

What most helped prevent offenses was a constant, predictable routine every single day. His life was so ordered to keep him engaged, there was no room for a chronic behavior problem. The routine we established is what saved us and helped us make it through each day. From the first day, we used a feeding and naptime routine and then expanded, as he grew, to playtime and activity routine. He was constantly held in the security of a predictable life.

It was always evident how important this routine was to Drew. If we went anywhere, he was always much worse in his behavior and anxiety

114

level. He just could not tolerate chaos or unpredictability. The worst thing I experienced at home with him was his aloofness and apparent lack of affection for me, as well as what appeared to be an oppositional reaction each time a demand was placed on him that he wasn't prepared for. Once again, the daily routine helped to curb this attitude of defiance towards me. Compliance was always expected and that was the message slowly being taught.

Even when we had believed Drew was normal, we knew it would be confusing to send a mixed message. We couldn't discipline him one day and not the next. Knowing Drew's state now made this rule all the more crucial.

The other important thing was that David and I worked as a team and frequently discussed our parenting methods. There were never any questions about what action needed to be taken for what offense. Drew's personality was so black and white, he added to the simplicity.

Drew lacked the ability to lie or deceive. His actions were always springing from his most present feelings. He was clear cut, which helped us, in a sense, to be consistent with him. He didn't seem to have the ability to deceive—to think ahead and plan his ways, to trick us and get what he wanted. He didn't seem to care what we might think or feel. He just expressed his immediate emotion. According to the books, this is the nature of autism: an inability to look outside oneself . . . to be self-absorbed, self-consumed. At first I wasn't sure if this wasn't simply a sin problem. Maybe it manifested itself to a greater degree in the autistic individual. Self-centeredness is present in all of us when we are born. There had to be some reason for this increased "curling in" of one's self that was so evident and consuming in the autistic.

I read and read to try to discover why. Plowing through the mountain of theories and speculation, I tried my best to make sense of it. Eventually, I determined that, no, this was not ultimately a spiritual problem but, rather, a physical one. This was not to say that he did not retain the spiritual problem we all share as sons of Adam. We are dead in our sins and in desperate need of a rebirth. We were forced to think Biblically and be guided supremely by the Scriptures. There was plenty of worldly wisdom to whisk us off in this direction or that. A phrase frequently uttered from the pulpit in our church ran through my mind: "Ultimately all things are disciplined by theology." How we viewed God and how we viewed man would be the guide to how we treated Drew's autism. We determined the following rules would be the basis to guide us in our approach:

- Rule number one: Drew's humanity never was altered because of his autism. We needed to maintain our view of him as a moral creature, created in the very image of God.
- Rule number two: Because of his nature, we were to use the Scriptures to direct how we should deal with him.

Elliot's and Drew's essence was identical—they were both moral beings. At the same time, Elliot and Drew were very different individuals as seen in their personalities and, of course, due especially to Drew's autism. But the required moral standard was the same for both.

What I needed help with was figuring out how Drew's brain worked, how he learned skills, how he processed and applied information. And thankfully, by God's common grace to mankind, He providentially bestowed at least part of this wisdom to some researchers in the field of autism. I learned that there was damage somewhere in the brain which caused a severe sensory perception problem and, sometimes, cognitive problems.

I began to understand the main approaches to autism. There is the psychoanalytical view with its various corresponding treatments; for example, the Option Institute, holding therapy, psychoanalysis, and play therapy. Then there is the very popular behaviorist approach which has been shown to be one of the most successful with its use of behavior modification (or Applied Behavior Analysis) techniques. And then there are the pharmacological treatments: the use of medications

116

to control undesired behavior. There is also the physiological approach, which includes sensory integration, auditory training, the organizing of the neurological system, diet, and even vitamin and nutritional therapies. The only treatments that have no proven record of efficacy in the treatment of autism are those therapies stemming from a psychoanalytical basis; however, there seems to be a portion of credibility with each of the other views listed. No one approach seemed perfect to us, though. None of them considered the moral essence of the child.

The psychotherapist would want to know the "why" behind the behavior of the autistic child. Not viewing him as a fallen creature in Adam, any aberrant behavior would somehow be linked to an environmental cause. This would be something inflicted on the child, generally by the mother. It could have occurred before birth, while still in the womb, or after birth while in the care of the cold and unloving mother. The lack of acceptance and love makes a child autistic, and their presence will ultimately bring him out of his autism.

The behaviorist doesn't care about the "whys," only the "what" of the here and now. The child performs an undesirable behavior and the goal is to blast it out of existence and replace it with a desirable behavior or skill. This technique functions with the use of rewards and punishments to shape and mold a child's outward behavior and the teaching of skills. This again denies the nature of the child who has been created in the image of God. Because he is a moral being, his training ought to go further than the mere restraining and reshaping of outward behavior. We need to pierce to the very core of his problem. His conscience needs to be trained in what is morally right and morally wrong. Whether the child learns right from wrong isn't an issue considered by the behaviorist. To him, the child is in a moral vacuum, like a dog.

The pharmacological approach has been shown to be helpful for some autistics because of the apparent chemical imbalance in the brain. Although a medication can address a symptom of the autistic syndrome, however, it doesn't provide real improvement in his brain.

What I call the physiological approach to autism—righting what is wrong in the brain through specific training and stimulation—seems to be the only treatment which attacks the very core of the problem. This is especially seen in the earliest years when there appears to be some ability to "re-circuit" the brain while it is still growing. Still, to provide a purely physiological approach is considering only physical health. By not taking into consideration the true state of the child's heart, and considering only his physical health, a parent is ignoring his first and foremost duty to his child.

15
He Is My God, Though Dark My Road

Nervously I opened the mailbox and found an envelope from the school district. It had been a couple of weeks since Drew's assessment. I was to be reminded, in print, of the official findings of that day. The nagging, sick feeling I had in the pit of my stomach the day of the testing returned. I ripped open the letter. My hands trembled. I fingered the important-looking yellow documents.

Confidential Summary of Assessments/Summary Analysis
Name: Drew Steere. Birthdate: 8-14-92. Sex: M.

My eyes scanned the papers in an effort to soak in as much as possible. The last sentence at the bottom of the final page summed up the whole report:

District Decision: Is the student eligible for special education program services as defined by the Washington Administrative Code? Yes _X_ No__.

There it was—by the experts' own advice, Drew qualified with a simple check mark after the word yes. It was actually the following phrase under the title of "funding category" that made me take in a sharp breath:

Developmentally Handicapped/Developmental Delay

The word *handicapped* made me shudder. Drew's sweet, innocent face came into my mind. I read the horrid word again, only this time whispering it in the space around me. I couldn't see how the two matched: that word with my Drew.

All hopes that the testing day was only a black nightmare quickly disintegrated with each utterance of the word "handicapped." No, it had really taken place—every bit of it. It wasn't just a dream. The proof of it lay in the three pieces of paper recklessly stapled together here in my hands.

Following is a summary of the report:

Recommendation of the multidisciplinary team for suggested educational programs and related services:

Specially designed classroom instruction/intervention in the areas of Pre-academic skills, receptive and expressive language, social skills, and self-help skills.

Direct specially designed instruction-related services to address needs in the area of communication.

Perceptual skills: Fine motor skills are currently within a normal range; however, he shows signs of tactile defensiveness and things had to be just so. Recommend rescreen at age four and a half.

Language/Communication: Peabody Picture Vocabulary Test receptive vocabulary age score of two years, six months, which when compared to actual age of three years, eleven months results in a standard deviation of two years, one month. Auditory comprehension: age two years, eleven months. Expressive communication: age two years, five months. Great difficulty processing information; answering questions. Echolalic

Academic: Disclosed an academic age of 29 months vs. a chronological age of 47 months. Drew tried hard. He was distractible and tired after previous testing in the day. He showed strength in perceptual discrimination. Conceptual development was severely delayed. Redirection from parents and me was ongoing.

Social/Emotional: The Vineland Adaptive Behavior Scales were completed in these areas with both parents reporting. Drew's self-help skills are delayed by two years, five months. Social skills are delayed by two years, seven months.

There it was. A neat and tidy package. I put the letter aside and cried, unable to shut the words out of my head. "Great difficulty." "Distractible." "Severely delayed." "Handicapped." Each word drove the dagger further and further into my heart and drained me of hope. I plunged deeper and deeper into the dreadful pit of despair. I felt left for dead with no strength to escape.

It was the end of July and another hot day. We were scheduled to meet with the pediatric neurologist for the official diagnosis. Leaving Elliot with Jayni once again, we left for the doctor's office. This event was not as earth-shaking as the testing by the school district. What more was there to learn? We had no doubt Drew was autistic. We simply wanted an expert to sanction our findings and send us on our way.

With each passing day that had led up to this doctor's visit I had read what I could about autism. I had compiled a list of things dredged up from my memory to share with the doctor. I wouldn't forget anything concerning Drew's past.

The office was in a bad section of the city, but upon entering the old building, we were surprised at how different the inside looked from the outside. The office was neat, clean, and orderly. Several desks held computers behind a long, tall desk that separated the office area from the waiting area. At each desk sat a woman busy typing and bustling about. We were given a clipboard with some papers attached and a pen. We went to a seating area to wait for the doctor. On the table next to our chairs were some out-of-date magazines and a dusty plastic plant. There were no toys.

I suppose handicapped children don't need toys, I thought.

David began filling out the paperwork. There was a drinking fountain attached to the opposite wall. Drew ran to it and began starting and stopping the water flow, turning the knob this way and that. After sitting for about fifteen minutes, we were joined by a young mother and her baby and what appeared to be her two-year-old boy. She was carrying a diaper bag and a familiar-looking clipboard. I stared impolitely at the little boy. He looked normal to me. He watched Drew who was now playing with the doorknob of the bathroom adjacent to the waiting room. My gazed shifted to her sleeping infant. Everyone in the room appeared normal . . . everyone, that is, but Drew. He had unstoppable energy and determination, going from drinking fountain to door knob to plastic plant. I was becoming irritated over the fact that we had now patiently waited forty-five minutes in a barren room with an autistic boy who had nothing to do. We had arrived ten minutes before our scheduled appointment knowing we would fill out paperwork. I scheduled what I thought was the first appointment of the day, 8:00 A.M., so that we could avoid having to sit and wait.

Finally Dr. Franken appeared with a file in his hands. "Drew Steere," he announced, sounding as though he was asking us a question.

"Yes," I rose, taking Drew's hand, relieved to finally get on with it.

We followed the white coat into his office. Dr. Franken was a gentle man and smiled when he introduced himself. He showed us a seat across from his expansive desk.

The room was somewhat dark and cold. It was orderly, with a loaded bookshelf behind the doctor's huge chair. The room had a dual purpose. Not only was it an office, but it appeared to be an examination room as well. There was an examination table covered with crinkly paper, a tall scale, and a small medicine cabinet in the corner. A doctor's black bag was sitting open on the examination table revealing a stethoscope on top. The doctor seemed far away when we all finally sat down, and I looked at him across his massive desk. I felt we were not alone when I spied a model of a brain near me on the edge of the desk.

"So you believe your son is autistic," began the doctor. He looked over the chart in his hands. "Tell me why you think so," he said, finally looking at us, ready for us to convince him.

"Well," I said, clearing my throat and pulling my handwritten pile of papers from my purse, "I wrote some things down so that I wouldn't forget anything."

"Wonderful," he said, smiling, and picked up a pen. "That should help a lot. Go ahead."

I began my litany, starting with Drew as a baby. I told how he screamed all of the time and could not be comforted. How he was stiff and pulled away when held. How there was no eye contact. How he hated the invasion of his space by others. How he preferred objects over people. How he seemed terrorized by elevators and the vacuum cleaner. How he didn't understand a group situation and acted like the others didn't exist. I told of his phenomenal memory skills, specifically concerning letters and numbers. How he read by three years but lacked in comprehension. I told how he loved wheels—anything that rolled. How he lined things up in perfect lines. How he became easily overwhelmed and screamed when his routine was changed. How he didn't speak until he was two and a half, and even then it was only single words. Even now, at nearly four years old, there was barely any reciprocal language. He echoed what we said or he said nothing at all. I told of his odd rituals—having to put Bear and his digital watch in a certain place before he ate or before bed.

On and on I went. I could feel my face getting warmer. The doctor sat across from me, madly taking notes. David quietly looked down, listening to the detailed description of his child. Drew was flitting about silently behind me, enamored with the mini-blinds, the scale, the books. He was innocently unaware of the weight this discussion held for him, of the death sentence about to be officially proclaimed upon him.

"That's everything I can think of," I said, looking up from my notes.

"That was very good," responded the doctor. He finished writing his last sentence.

He rose, chose a large red book from the bookshelf behind him, and opened it.

"Tell me if you think this fits him."

He began to slowly read off a list of symptoms which he felt applied to Drew. David and I looked at each other and shrugged with a nod of agreement.

"This is the youngest case of Asperger's I have ever seen," said Dr. Franken as he studied Drew from across the room.

"What is Asperger's?" we asked.

"It's a form of high-functioning autism," came the simplified answer. "He is unbelievably well behaved," he added.

I was surprised that I felt nothing at this announcement. No tears, no pain, no shock. It was all so matter of fact. No scary medical tests to put Drew through and wait for results on. No CAT scan, no blood test, no lab work. Just three adults sitting around a textbook and subjectively agreeing on a label.

The doctor took a couple of minutes to test Drew's reflexes and see if he could balance on one foot. Nothing very technical. Nothing we couldn't have just told him over the phone.

Returning to his mighty throne behind the desk which, to me, symbolized the huge cavern which existed between parent and professional, he gave a treatment plan.

"I'm prescribing Anafranil, a drug used to treat obsessive compulsive disorder."

He scribbled his autograph on the bottom of the prescription pad, ripped it off, and handed it to me.

"What?" I asked, bewildered.

"I have watched him return to that scale several times. Normally, a child would investigate it once and then move on to something else. Based on this repeated activity and the things you described, I'm sure you would see him benefit from this drug." He went on to tell of another young patient of his whose life had drastically changed for the better because of this drug.

"Well," I stammered, "I wasn't expecting this. I'd like to read something about it first."

"That's fine," he said. "I'll have one of the girls make you some copies from the PDR [Physicians' Desk Reference] that will tell you of side effects and any adverse reactions."

124

Adverse reactions, I thought. *He's only four years old!*

The doctor then wrote down the name of an office that we could take Drew to, perhaps once a week, for sensory integration therapy. That was it. Nothing more. I supposed that since we came in saying the word autism, he thought we didn't fear it, despise it, that we had even accepted it. Although he seemed kind and attentive, he delivered everything to us very clinically and objectively. How ironic that he should display such objectivity when a diagnosis was obtained so subjectively.

Before we left, we handed a large sum of money over to the lady in the billing department. I felt cheated having to pay for something we had already figured out on our own and for something as ugly as autism. Autism, so debilitating, so hopeless, so chronic. If we had been given the diagnosis of cancer, we would have been handled much more gently and much more sensitively. None of this "Take this pill and go get therapy once a week." Thanks a lot for nothing.

As I continued to talk with parents of autistic children over the phone, I was introduced to an important name: Dr. Bernard Rimland, the founder of the Autism Research Institute in Southern California. The parent of an autistic child himself, he became one of my most treasured resources. After calling the institute and requesting a parent information packet, I received one in the mail only days later. Excitedly, I opened the thick envelope. It was refreshing to read of responsible research being done in the area of autism. The information that struck me as the most helpful was the data on vitamin therapy. After receiving Dr. Franken's prescription for Anafranil and reading of all its side effects, it was not hard for David and me to consider using vitamin therapy with Drew. Rimland wrote that in comparison to drug treatment, very infrequently, if ever, were there any reports of side effects. He went on to say that if the vitamin therapy were to show some success in an autistic individual, it would be because the individual in question was in need of extra amounts of those vitamins.

Continuing, he said that while drugs simply suppress symptoms, vitamins are given to facilitate the natural metabolism in individuals who have a much larger than normal need for these nutrients. So the vitamins may work or they may not. We saw nothing to lose for trying them—it could be just what Drew needed.

We ordered some vitamins and anxiously awaited their arrival, hoping they just might be the miracle cure. While waiting for our "cure" to come, I read the papers over and over again: "We have found vitamin B_6 and the mineral magnesium to be helpful in nearly 50 percent of the children studied. Our results have been strongly confirmed by a number of other investigators, and now there are eighteen published studies which confirm our finding that vitamin B_6 and magnesium are helpful in many cases of autism."

I read and reread the materials, almost memorizing them. "The benefits which are most often observed in autistic children given B_6 and the accompanying nutrients are: increased use of sounds, words, or speech; improved sleeping habits; decrease in hyperactivity and irritability; better attention span; increase in interest in learning. In some cases, self-stimming, self-injurious, and/or assaultive behaviors have decreased. Vitamin B_6 makes the child more normal, in many ways. Other benefits reported have included such indications of improved health as better skin color and complexion, and better muscle tone. Many parents say their child has never been in better health."

More normal with B_6, I repeated to myself. Normal—what a wonderful word. This surely is the answer for finding our lost Drew.

When the vitamins arrived the next week, I served Drew some with his dinner. He was to receive a portion of the daily dosage at each meal. I also included a food nutrient called DMG, which was to make the B_6 even more effective in the body.

The clicking sound of the spoon whipping up the concoction in a little cup of applesauce was music to my ears. Matter-of-factly, I

126

approached Drew's mouth with a spoonful of the wonder "cure."

"Lick it all off," I said, turning the spoon around so Drew wouldn't miss even a speck of vitamin.

Obediently Drew opened his mouth as he had been trained to do a long while back.

"Ohhhhh," he reacted as his face twisted with disgust.

I was prepared for this to not be very tasty, but Drew took it anyway as he was instructed.

"Hurray—good job!" I kissed him happily on the cheek. "What a good job. You obeyed Mommy and opened your mouth!"

I swiftly provided him with a plate of spaghetti—his favorite.

Cleaning up the kitchen, I intently watched Drew as he ate, longing for any telltale sign of recovery. *What was that?* I hoped to myself. *Did he make eye contact with me?*

I really didn't know exactly what I was waiting to see after only one little spoonful of vitamins, but I was wanting something really big.

Rinsing off some plates in the sink and watching the suds swirl down the drain, I imagined Drew bursting forth with verbiage as never heard from him before. That's what all the papers had said, "Increased use of sounds, words or speech . . . more normal in many ways."

The only thing I heard was the tapping of his utensil against the side of his dish as he finished up, scraping each and every last noodle. The rest of the evening was just as silent as usual, punctuated only by fits of frustration exploding now and then. No miraculous healing, no instant recovery, no cure. I went to bed that night a little disappointed but at least more realistic. I was rudely reminded once again of the nature of the monster. It just doesn't go away—and I have to expect that it probably never will.

Another helpful resource provided by Dr. Rimland and the research institute was the E2 checklist. This checklist was designed to help in the process of diagnosing children who have been given a label of autistic, autistic-like, PDD (Pervasive Developmental Disorder), severely atypical, childhood schizophrenia, or any similar or related label. David and I filled out the questionnaire and sent it into the institute. It was free and more comprehensive for obtaining a diagnosis than anything we had yet been given or asked by any professional. I was surprised at how quickly we received the results. Drew received a score of +1 for behavior and +8 for speech. The total score was +9. I read the information included with the score to try to understand what these numbers meant. The following is an explanation of the meaning of the numbers:

The scores on Form E2 range from -45 (lowest) to +45 (highest). The average score on Form E2 for a child diagnosed as "autistic" by professionals around the world is -2. Children who score from -15 to +19 are typically regarded as "autistic" by professionals worldwide. The vast majority of children diagnosed as autistic fall within this range.

Drew certainly fell within the range for autism. Despite the score, we felt more confident now that we had this diagnostic opinion drawn from a detailed format.

After immersing ourselves in information on Asperger's for another week, David and I disagreed with Dr. Franken's diagnosis. If I had only had a little more knowledge before seeing him, I would have been able to ensure a more accurate diagnosis and not so readily accepted Asperger's as the right one. There was a reason for Dr. Franken to be amazed at Drew, the youngest Asperger's case he had ever seen, because Drew didn't fit into that category. Two of the defining characteristics of someone with Asperger's are that it is usually not recognized before thirty months of age, and speech is not delayed as in most autistic children. Both of these characteristics were found in Drew. Drew's problems were from birth—the stiff, unrelatable, screaming infant, the delay in language. Drew didn't even use single words until between two and a half and three years old.

Our visit with the all-knowing, expert neurologist was seeming more and more a waste of time and money. We were beginning to see, despite Drew's actual score or label, that the same treatment plan was suggested for all. Autistic children need an early, intensive, one-on-one educational approach in a well-structured and positive learning environment. That's all that really mattered at this time anyway. Enough of trying to determine the exact "what" our son had, or even the "how" he had gotten it. No one could really know either of these things for sure. What stared us in the face was our lack of time. The sense of urgency was overwhelming. So much valuable time had been wasted. It was a mad rush to figure out the best treatment and to begin as soon as possible.

16
What Though I Can't His Goings See

Although Drew was intense, we felt we had control over him. Our daily maintenance of minute-by-minute routine continued. This held life together and kept it and Drew's behavior from spinning out of control. The area we saw the most need for help in was language. I learned the professional term used to describe the way Drew communicated. It was referred to as "echolalic." Instead of interacting in dialogue with us, Drew simply repeated our questions back to us. He was unable to answer a simple "yes" or "no" question. Screaming and crying were the verbal replacement for the word no. There wasn't any reciprocal communication at all with Drew at four years old. He was able to identify most objects if we pointed to them around the house: chair, table, book, bed, etc. But he remained mostly silent and distant.

He was obsessed with fingering objects, riding his rocking horse, or listening to music and typing letters on his computer. We continued to force him to listen to the picture books read to him hours each day, and we insisted he follow through on a command, even if that meant physically walking him through it, directing his body through the desired task.

"Mommy said come here," I would gently say in his ear while walking backwards, pulling his arms toward me. "Good job—you came to Mommy."

No matter what he was doing, I tried to interact even though he rarely looked at me.

"You are sitting very nicely." "You are running fast." "You are eating your sandwich." "You are going potty." "You waited very patiently."

My one-sided relationship with Drew pressed on. It was the only option we had—to keep pressing on. To not press on meant losing Drew to a place far more unreachable. I hoped that maybe, just maybe, he would understand or relate back. We just kept talking at that blank, hollow little expressionless face.

So many books I had read on autism described out of control, wild children. I felt we were hanging by a thin, fragile thread; if it broke, we would easily have an aggressive, completely self-consumed child who was out of control. Again, it was routine that kept us afloat. Drew wasn't regressing or progressing. I was happy we were at least maintaining a level. My reading revealed what life with an autistic child could be like, and I saw that it could easily be much, much worse!

Our biggest concern was the development of Drew's ability to speak and use language appropriately. Our scheduled days took care of behavior, but we knew we needed some expert help in the area of communication. I called my pediatrician for a referral to a speech pathologist. He readily recommended one nearby and I called to set up an appointment. I couldn't wait to begin.

It was a beautiful August morning as David, Drew, and I drove over the Narrows Bridge to go and meet with Becky Bier*, the speech pathologist.

"Look at the beautiful water. Can you see the boats down there?" I asked Drew, not expecting a response. I turned around to look at the quiet figure all alone in the backseat. Drew was looking out the window at the blue expanse below. His eyes were as blue as the water, but lacked the calmness of the water beneath us. His stiff, erect body leaned in the direction of his window, his lips parted slightly and his head cocked to one side. The railing of the mile-long bridge over Puget Sound was racing past us in a flutter as we drove to Becky Bier's office. I felt more relaxed about leaving Elliot with Jayni, positive of the fun time they would share. I even thought I had a slight sense of joy mixed with excitement within myself. Today was a beginning. A moving forward. We were actually doing something positive in the direction of

---

* Name has been changed to protect identity.

fixing what was wrong with Drew. We were out of what I thought was the darkest period. From the revelation of a problem, the deliberation of what it was and what to do about it, we had progressed to the annihilation of that problem. Drew was going to get some help from someone who knew how to help him.

We pulled into the parking lot surrounded by a long, meandering building of offices and shops. Getting out of the car, I let the sun touch my back for a moment. Its warmth matched the mood of my heart.

"C'mon honey—hold my hand in the parking lot," I said, holding my hand out to Drew.

He didn't reach for my hand, so I took his. "Good. You're holding Mommy's hand. Good job."

I took my sunglasses off when we entered the small waiting room. It took a while for my eyes to become accustomed to the dim room. The atmosphere was soothing with its cool air and huge potted plants. Soft music played. We stood alone at the little window in the waiting room. A woman appeared behind the desk and handed David a clipboard and motioned to us to have a seat. "Becky Bier will be out shortly," she smiled.

David and I took seats in the small, empty waiting room. Drew was drawn like a magnet to some Legos and other small toys placed neatly on a shelf in the corner. While David filled out the required paperwork, Drew played intently on the floor, and I waited with excited anticipation for the entrance of the "savior."

After only a few minutes, a door near the shelf of toys swung open and in entered Becky Bier, speech pathologist. She was a small-framed woman in her forties, dressed tastefully in a tan silk blouse and pants. Clunky jewelry hung from her ears and neck. Her dark hair was swooped up and held in random order. A warm, broad smile greeted us with a squeeze of her hand. "Hi," she said. "Everyone just calls me Bier." She instantly put me at ease.

"This must be Drew," she declared, glancing down at Drew who remained fixated upon some rolling Legos despite her entrance.

After asking us some additional questions about insurance, she told us it was time to take Drew to the back with her.

"I'd like to watch," I said, standing and taking Drew's hand.

This must have been an unusual request, for there was a moment of bustle to find an additional chair to squeeze into the tiny room at the end of the hall. David remained out in the waiting room because of lack of space.

The little room was jam-packed with all sorts of teaching materials and toys. Bier showed Drew a small chair to sit in at a short table in the corner. She pulled a similar chair under herself and scooted toward the table. I clicked my pen and prepared to take notes on everything I witnessed so that I could duplicate the "healer's" techniques at home.

Bier had a childish manner and an almost clown-like expression on her face. Her earrings made a clicking sound when her head nodded praise whenever Drew performed just right. "Good job! Aren't you smart!" She giggled when Drew repeated an appropriate phrase for her.

She held a small car in one hand and a miniature Big Bird in the other. Drew definitely wanted the car. "Ohhh Nooo!" Drew said, trying to grab the car she was holding out to him.

"Say, 'I want car.' "

"I want car," yelled a panicky Drew.

Bier relinquished the car into Drew's possession and immediately a relaxed expression came over his face. He rolled the car across the tabletop.

"Good talking," said Bier with an oversized smile.

She turned to me after more similar exercises and spoke as if sharing highly confidential information. "My! You can really tell he's been worked with at home."

My heart swelled. I watched Drew playing with some puzzle pieces. I didn't know how she was able to discern our efforts, but I was so happy to have some recognition from a professional. We had done something right for our child. Of course these words of encouragement made me fall in love with Bier.

I madly wrote down ideas to use with Drew at home as I watched Bier work. She emphasized putting language in receptively. Whatever I saw Drew doing, I was to say it.

"You are eating." "You are drinking." "You are riding in the car." "You are taking a bath."

The other thing I wrote down was the sequence of items we would work on first:

1. "What" questions; for example, "What is this?" Drew could already do this pretty well from the many hours of reading picture books at home.

2. "Where" questions; for example, "Where is the book?" Bier was happy to see that he did fairly well in this area, too. Once again, I knew it was from reading.

3. "When" questions; for example, "When do we eat?" These questions were beyond Drew. "Do you eat?" he repeated.

"Why" and "how" questions would be worked on after the others were mastered. It seemed it would be in the far off future before Drew could understand these kinds of questions.

It didn't really matter right now, though. We were on the road to recovery.

Bier showed me how I could use a ball and sit across from Drew on the floor to help teach the my turn/your turn concept. Rolling the ball to Drew, Bier said, "Your turn."

Drew picked up the ball and began to inspect it, not understanding the idea of returning it to Bier.

"Say, 'My turn,' " said Bier while moving Drew's hand through the motion of rolling the ball back to herself.

Although nothing seemed very technical to me, I began to see how I could incorporate some simple teaching games into our day to help

Drew use language. Some things we had already been doing, like not giving Drew what he wanted until he asked for it the right way.

Our half-hour session flew by and we found ourselves at the door saying goodbye to Bier. She was the one. She was going to show us how to find words in Drew.

Several days later we received a copy of a letter Bier had sent to our pediatrician:

> Dear Dr. Markey:
>
> Thank you for referring Drew Steere to me for evaluation and treatment of speech and language function. Drew came to me on August 5, 1996, to begin the evaluation process. Mr. and Mrs. Steere provided me with historical information concerning Drew's language delay, indicating that Tacoma Public Schools' assessment in Child Find in July indicated that Drew was functioning at a two and one-half year level in speech and language acquisition. Also, I am informed that Dr. Carl Franken is following Drew in the area of neurological development.
>
> I will be continuing Drew's assessment in speech and language acquisition over the next few weeks. Initial impression suggests that Drew exhibits a specific central speech and language disturbance rather than the more typical developmental delay in speech and language acquisition. Accompanied with this language disturbance, and as significant, is Drew's atypical and delayed social development. Receptively, Drew's echolalia, delay in response, and limited but stereotypical responses, indicate a disturbance in processing spoken language. Expressively, Drew's pronoun errors, use of own name, flat intonation pattern, and somewhat limited and repetitive vocal repertoire indicate Drew's difficulty in use of spoken language

for social pragmatics. On the other hand, I was impressed with Drew's strength in visual and spatial areas, in memory, and in his high motivation to communicate. Treatment plan is to use this strength in visual learning to assist development of verbal language. This technique is helpful with children with Hyperlexia or Asperger's Syndrome (this information obtained by neurologist), as well as any visual learner.

I will keep you updated regarding our program. Please do not hesitate to ask me for more information, or to send me information that could help in my treatment with Drew.

Sincerely,

Becky Bier, M.A.,C.C.C., Speech-Language Pathologist

❖ ❖ ❖

David and I were aware that Drew needed more help than the half-hour session with Bier once every other week. We felt that precious time had already been wasted by getting a diagnosis so late in his life. I was still contacting mothers I had heard about through word of mouth. There was a number I hadn't tried yet of a mother in California with an autistic daughter. I dialed her up one evening, not knowing that this call would provide the solution to our dilemma. After only a few rings a friendly sounding voice answered. I told her how I had obtained her number and asked her about her daughter.

"I'm so glad you called," she began. "I'd love to tell you about Michelle. We've been having such success with her."

My ears perked up. No one yet had sounded so optimistic or hopeful. "So what are you doing with her?" I wanted to know.

"Michelle just turned five, and for the past two years we have been doing a home program with her, designed by the National Academy for Child Development. She has made astounding progress."

This all sounded too good to be true—I clung to her every word. For the next hour this woman whom I had never met handed me the key to unlock Drew from his autism. The following day I contacted NACD and anxiously awaited their material's arrival in our mailbox. The day the information arrived I was shaking with excitement. I opened the brochure on top and began to read:

NACD embraces five basic concepts:

1. Foremost is the belief that every child has unlimited potential.
2. NACD believes that the parent is the single, most important element in the child's development. No one knows a child better than the parent, and there is no substitute for the one-to one parent/child relationship.
3. We believe the more a family can work with the child, the more progress he or she will make.
4. Schools and professionals should play a supportive, as opposed to primary, role in the child's development.
   We believe the key is to give parents the necessary technical and educational tools to do the bulk of the work themselves. This self-sufficiency model is both effective and cost efficient and totally in keeping with the changing attitudes toward education in this country.
5. This principle involves the child's right to eclectic treatment and assistance. A child with a problem needs to have access to everything that can help. Parents are rarely aware that educators, therapists, and other professionals often represent narrowly specific approaches, and to most professionals "doing everything possible" really only means doing all that exists within their often limited or restricted approach.

I became more excited the more I read. This sounded like the perfect answer; I couldn't wait to show David the material when he got home from work that night. Up until this point, the only other option we saw was the very popular—and documented as the most successful—approach of Behavior Modification (or ABA). They had the numbers to prove their success—recovering nearly half of all children. Even though David and I had problems on a philosophical basis with behavior modification, we saw it as a tool we could use and modify to our own liking if this was a proven method for helping the autistic child learn. Nothing else offered hope . . . until now with NACD.

David and I went back and forth in our minds. Which would we use? Whatever we chose carried the weight of Drew's entire future. We discussed the pros and cons of each option deep into the night. We would sway from one opinion to another, landing on one until persuaded differently by arguments in favor of the other. Getting dizzy with indecision, we decided we had only our intellect and ultimately our trust in a sovereign God to help us decide. We could see how making this kind of a decision could lead us to act like the modern-day religious person who was always seeking signs and wonders. Yes, it would be easier to lay out the fleece or search for the handwriting on the wall. That wasn't God's way, though. We were created in His image and given a mind to consider and ponder and weigh the consequences of a situation. We don't live by instinct like animals—we have a mind to think and reason. So that's what we did, and then we prayed to our God and asked for His grace and wisdom and blessing. And He answers prayer . . .

We made the decision to go with NACD.

I felt that a heavy load had been lifted. I dialed the Seattle branch of the National Academy for Child Development (NACD) to make an appointment. After talking with a quiet but friendly voice on the line, I was about to hang up when I heard her say something that shattered my hopes like a piece of fine china hitting the cement.

"What did you say?" I asked, beginning to panic.

"We'll send you the paperwork and after you fill it out and send it back to us, we'll set up an appointment for you to meet with Bob Doman in Utah," came the reply.

"I didn't know we would have to go to Utah," I said, starting to lose control.

"Oh yes," came the calm voice. "Everyone meets with Bob for the initial evaluation."

Suddenly, visual images began to bombard me—making me feel more nauseated as the implications of this news sank in. How could we possibly afford all of this: the air fare on top of the cost of the evaluation? I couldn't even picture getting on an airplane with Drew. How could I ever leave Elliot overnight?

Our choice to go with NACD was beginning to look more and more bleak. After a brief moment of silence, the lady suggested going ahead and sending her the paperwork anyway. On some rare occasions, after NACD looked over the history of the child, the local consultant had been granted authority to perform the initial intake evaluation. It was a speck of shimmering hope in the sudden darkness that enshrouded me. I wanted to cry out after hanging up the phone, "Don't you know how hard it was for us to reach this decision? Doesn't anyone care?"

Time was running out and we felt like rats trapped in a maze, turning this way and bumping headlong into the wall; turning that way and hitting another dead end. There appeared no way out. Meanwhile, lost and lonely, Drew waited. We had to find the way out for him. All we could do was get up, shove the burning, hot tears back, and continue our mad scurry.

Our momentum had been slowed, but not halted. When the paperwork arrived from NACD, we filled it out and sent it back. Our prayer was that God would be pleased to work things out so that we would not have to travel to Utah. The ringing phone made me jump.

"Hello. Yes, this is Cathy." My pulse quickened. I was about to find out if NACD was our answer or not.

"Well—I faxed your paperwork to Utah." I could sense her smile. "And they gave permission for me to do the evaluation here in Seattle."

"Oh—thank you, thank you, thank you!" I cried into the receiver.

I heard a chuckle in response to my dramatics. "I thought that would make you happy," she said.

Before hanging up we set up an appointment for a couple of weeks away.

First right, then left. Now open space before me. No more walls to stop me.

I'm coming, baby—Mommy's found the way out!

We returned to Bier the following Monday. I didn't want to give her up. She agreed to see us on a consultation basis. We simply could not afford the twice a week, half-hour sessions. Unfortunately, we had discovered insurance didn't cover this type of therapy, because autism was listed under "mental illness." So whenever we had fifty dollars, we scheduled an appointment with Bier while I wildly took notes on a pad of yellow legal paper.

I was anxious to tell Bier about our acceptance with NACD.

"Mmmm—I've never heard of them," she said, furrowing her brow after I told her the news.

Her response didn't set well with me. Surely, she should know about this international organization helping so many autistic children. With great fervor, I began a speech about NACD, hoping something I would say would jar her memory and she would respond with a reassuring, "Ah, yes! I have heard about them. What a good decision."

Instead the furrow didn't leave her brow and her face wore a look of concern. I concluded my feeble words of praise for this organization we were about to put all of our trust in. I could tell she was choosing her words very carefully when she finally did speak. "It all sounds very interesting," she graciously offered, "but there's another place I'd like you to consider first."

I felt a little defensive because of all of the turmoil we had gone through already. How flippantly she tossed this new consideration to us. Weren't the dark circles under our eyes enough of a sign that this decision hadn't been easily reached? I finally decided that it wouldn't be prudent to shut out any possibility and it wouldn't hurt to look.

Her demeanor quickly changed when she took the floor. She spoke candidly about an office of occupational therapists right around the corner, which offered sensory integration therapy. Many of Bier's "kids" received OT therapy once a week along with speech therapy. "You should see the wonderful results," she insisted with a nod of her head. Her earrings tinkled.

Yes, I was interested in observing this sensory integration therapy. I had read about it. It was settled. Next Monday I was to arrive at Bier's office and we would walk over to watch the "experts" at work.

It was now fall. The sun was shining and the air was cool and crisp. I didn't know whether I was more excited over observing the magical therapy session or over getting to see another child like Drew. I still had an insatiable desire to watch another autistic child and to see how Drew compared.

Bier was all warmth and smiles when she greeted me in her office the following Monday morning. "I think you'll really like what you see," she said with enthusiasm. She put on a sweater and we stepped outside.

We walked past several offices and rounded a corner to the back of the complex. We entered a buzzing little darkened waiting room filled with people. A giant mural of tall, creeping trees painted all over the walls gave me the feeling I had just entered a magical forest. Every chair was taken by an adult absorbed in a book or magazine. In the center of the room was a play area loaded with toys. Several young boys who looked about Drew's age or a couple of years older, were playing vigorously. I stopped short when I heard a familiar sound. "Ohhh nooo! Do you want that?" screeched a young voice.

Although I had never heard that particular voice before, it sounded eerily familiar. The panic and desperation, the very evident pronoun reversal. It took my brain a moment to register that this cry, although a familiar sound, wasn't coming from a familiar source. It was as if I had been transported to another planet. I was the alien. This was Drew's planet, with his "kind." I was surrounded by the noises of autism which in this setting seemed the norm rather than an oddity. I stood frozen as if in a dreamland. So there really were others like him. The jumble of Drew-speak which floated around my head forced tears into my eyes instead of bringing comfort to my heart. I wanted to run from this horrid place with these mixed-up noises.

My body went through the motions of following Bier through a side door of the waiting area. The confused voices were shut out behind the closed door behind me. I felt tired.

"This is Debbie." Bier motioned to a large blonde woman getting up to greet me. "You'll be watching her son receive therapy this morning."

I heard myself thank Debbie for letting me observe her son and watched my hand shake hers. My mind was stuck in a fog. It must not have shown, though, because everyone acted natural—although I didn't hear their words when they spoke to me.

The next thing I remember was sitting on a stool staring at a faint reflection of my own face in the glass of a one-way mirror. I tried to focus and concentrate on what was happening on the other side of the mirror. I couldn't hear anything, but I had a pretty good position from which to observe. Like the waiting room, the therapy room was dimly lit. I watched two young women dressed in T-shirts and stretch pants gently roll a huge inflated ball back and forth. Lying across the top of the ball was a boy about a year older than Drew with tousled dark hair. He was laughing as he swayed. Suddenly, the boy jumped down and ran over to the opposite wall where a mirror was attached. The two therapists bounded after him, seeming to know what he was expecting. One of the women squirted a blob of shaving cream into his little hand. The boy began to vigorously smear the cream all over the mirror in front of him, clouding his own reflection. The therapist imitated the boy and smeared the white foam in swirls next to him.

After tiring of this activity, the boy flitted over to a table where he wiped his hands on a towel and grabbed a tray that was filled with holes. The other therapist was instantly at his side to attend to his desire. He began to stick tiny pegs into each hole until he tired of that. Next, he ran to a huge piece of stretchy material hanging from the ceiling and draped like a hammock. The boy swung the material. Obeying his wish, the women hoisted him into the make-shift hammock. Back and forth, back and forth they rocked him. Everyone looked happy. Nobody looked cured.

I sat, feeling empty. The therapy session began wrapping up. Everyone tumbled out of the room. The young boy ran to Debbie who was sticking the novel she had been reading into her bag. "Did you have fun?" she asked the boy.

No eye contact. No answer. She didn't act surprised. I thanked her again before they left.

I found myself surrounded by the two therapists and Bier. They all looked expectantly at me for my favorable response to their product.

"So what did you think?" asked one of the occupational therapists. She was a bit out of breath from the hoops she had just finished jumping through for the boy.

"It was a real eye opener . . . " I stammered.

Taking that as a good thing, she smiled and finally caught her breath.

I continued, "What I would like to know is your opinion of the National Academy for Child Development." I thought that certainly these professionals could give me some answers to help me understand my options better.

I noticed a quick glance pass between the OT and Bier before Bier looked down at the floor. With confidence, as if prepared for my question, the OT answered, "The best way I can describe the National Academy and how they differ from us is to first tell you what our philosophy is."

That was good, I thought. *What is your philosophy?* I waited with bated breath. She obviously had something to say.

"We believe," she began, stressing the *we*, "that the child should be the one to guide the therapy. Who knows better than the child what he wants to do and what he doesn't want to do? When you force the brain to be stimulated, it just shuts down and there is no improvement. The brain just becomes overloaded." She seemed satisfied she had told me something that I, as a modern-day mother, would want to hear. She finished with her chin tilted slightly upward as if in a victory pose.

Little did she know that she and this whole place were turning me off more and more each moment. Next, she leaned toward Bier. I was beginning to see they were great friends. They most likely supplied clients for each other's businesses. She said in almost a whisper of secrecy, "I personally had one mother pull her child out of our therapy to use NACD."

"What happened?" exclaimed Bier almost as if on cue.

"I heard the child screamed the whole time and hated it," the OT snickered to Bier.

Bier shook her head with a knowing look of disapproval at this last statement and then looked at me as if to say, "Well, there you have it!"

I was happy to leave the planet I had mistakenly landed on. I hated it there. On the way out I noticed a poster hanging on the wall promoting the First Lady's new book *It Takes a Village.* If this was the village that was supposed to help Drew, I didn't want their help. Drew didn't belong on this planet any more than I did. Drew lived in our world and any help that was truly "help" would help him learn to live in it with us.

I left Bier that day more sure than ever that we had made the right choice to go with NACD. It disturbed me to see an injured child placed

144

in the position of deciding how his therapy should be conducted. This mentality was completely the opposite of how we approached Drew. It would have been like asking him, "So which parenting style would you prefer us to use with you, Drew?"

I can almost be assured of his answer: "The permissive parenting style of course, Ma! What else?"

We couldn't see handing the reins of control over to a "normal" child. The potential disaster was so evident. How much more ridiculous to let my confused, lost, autistic child determine what was best for himself. How could he possibly know?

17
He Holds Me That I Shall Not Fall

I actually felt happy as we drove to Seattle the morning of Drew's initial evaluation with NACD. Drew had just turned four years old a month before, but the addition of another birthday didn't make him appear any less vulnerable or fearful of the chaotic world around him. Knowing Elliot was again in Jayni's watchful care made me relax and concentrate on the day before us. The dark, dank pit of despair into which I had fallen head-long only weeks before didn't feel quite so cold today. I no longer felt the uncontrolled speed of the fall, which had plunged me into the grip of grief. My descent had, at least for the moment, ceased. I felt safe.

David turned our car into the parking lot of an old church building. We were fifteen minutes early and saw only two other cars in the lot. The building made me nervous. The unkempt appearance of the property, the overgrown lawn, and broken shades halfway down some of the windows made me shudder.

"Oh my," I whispered. "Are we at the right place?"

"Yep," said David, equally reluctant.

I remembered being told that our consultant used a church building to conduct evaluations when she traveled from her office in Spokane to Seattle. I was not prepared for the looks of the free accommodations to look so . . . free.

After parking, we slowly emerged from the car. David and I kept eyeing the facilities, hoping for some indication we were not at the right place after all. Suddenly, a tall woman in her thirties rounded the corner of the building and approached us.

"Hi," she said warmly, reaching to shake our hands. "You must be the Steeres. I'm Cyndi Ringoen with NACD. I'll be conducting Drew's evaluation."

We both greeted her in return. Within moments the looks of the place became insignificant and the focus of our journey pushed to the forefront of my thoughts. Cyndi's matter-of-fact demeanor and competent persona put me at ease instantly. Only after entering the building did I feel some hesitation. She told Drew to come with her to a separate room. David and I were to wait in an empty classroom next door. When Drew, not used to leaving us to go with a stranger, gave us a quick glance before heading off with her, I tried to relax and felt unusually trusting.

David and I sat, me trying not to wring my hands, as we waited for Drew. Nervously, I stood to pace the worn carpet and strained to hear something, anything, coming from the room next door. I was sure we would hear Drew's familiar scream sooner or later. All we heard was a "Good job!" from Cyndi punctuating the silence.

It seemed like forever had passed before Cyndi asked David and me in to talk. We followed her next door where Drew was quietly playing with a digital clock. I still couldn't get over the fact that Drew was so "calm" with this whole process. Cyndi acted as though she knew just how to handle him.

"May I please have that back now?" she asked him in a matter of fact manner and held her hand out.

Drew obeyed her instantly and moved on to some of his own objects of interest which we had brought along to occupy him. It was obvious Drew felt comfortable with this woman and he even, in his own way, seemed to like her.

David and I sat opposite Cyndi at a long table in a room that matched the rest of the place.

"How did he do?" I wanted desperately to know.

"Very well," came her genuine reply. Cyndi tucked her long hair behind her ear. "He is so well behaved," she smiled right into my eyes.

"He is?" I questioned, thinking I wasn't hearing quite right.

"Oh yes." She went on, watching Drew play with some cars on the yellow stained couch. "I've worked with many children, with the same difficulties as his, that are completely out of control. I'm very impressed."

David and I smiled at each other. I tried to restrain a happy tear from rolling down my cheek. If this woman only knew how encouraging those words were to us! All of the effort that the past few years had been filled with, trying to be as consistent as possible training Drew to a standard of obedience and self-control, came spilling into my mind. We hadn't known how horrendously difficult it ultimately was for Drew to learn, due to his problems . . . but he had learned.

For the next hour she discussed her findings with us and asked whether we thought they seemed accurate or not. Drew had been evaluated in the areas of tactility, auditory, visual, manual, language, and mobility. Cyndi tried to explain Drew's strengths and weaknesses in each area.

We were happy to hear she had tested Drew in the area of scholastic ability as well—something the school system hadn't even considered. Drew scored at nearly the beginning of a first grade level for math and nearly a second grade level for reading. I couldn't help but think of all the hours sitting with Drew on his bed, showing him how to sound out simple words. Also, I envisioned him playing with the wooden puzzle pieces, placing the numbers carefully on the floor.

We came away from our first evaluation with NACD with a sense of encouragement over the positive aspects of Drew's development. Feeling empowered and brimming with hope, we looked to a future of helping Drew conquer in the areas in which he was deficient.

Pulling out of the church parking lot, I glanced back at the building and surrounding property. It symbolized the disarray and confusion of Drew's perception of the world. It reflected the unorganized manner in which he processed information. *Don't worry, little guy,* I thought. *We've found the tools to help fix you up.*

A week later we received a home program designed specifically for

Drew. Each exercise was to address a certain weakness. The program included activities in the areas of fine and gross motor skills, language and communication skills, visual and auditory processing, and academic improvement. There would be exercises to improve short- and long-term memory abilities and to provide a general overall organization of his neurological system. The approach was eclectic and specific in nature. Included was a videotape of Cyndi telling and showing us exactly how to carry out these simple exercises.

The exercises themselves were not difficult or technical, but they were specific and needed to be applied consistently to bear any fruit. Sensory integration was seen as a crucial treatment for autistic children. The difference between the chaotic, "playtime" therapy I had witnessed and the sensory integration therapy we were going to provide Drew at home was as simple as the "how" of applying it. The key wasn't, "*Should* we apply sensory integration or should we not," but, "*How* should it be applied?"

The following is NACD's philosophy:

NACD's perception of the autistic child follows the neurological/sensory model. A child who has been labeled as "autistic" is viewed not as an emotionally disturbed child, or as a child with a psychiatric problem, but as a child with sensory dysfunction whose abnormal behavior is a reflection of abnormal perception.

We were beginning to see the importance of philosophy. If one held to a particular premise or presupposition, the therapy prescribed and the way it should be administered would be affected. For instance, if someone believed autism to be of a psychological origin, psychoanalysis would be the treatment of choice. Even so, that person might agree that the origin of autism is a neurological/sensory one. But as I learned by observing Bier's OT friends administer sensory therapy, a theological presupposition was made about children which was in error. Their view of the nature of the child prevented the therapy—which was in and of itself helpful—from being of any true value. The Scriptures do not endorse the notion that a child will naturally choose what is proper and upright, because of the condition of his lost and depraved heart. According to his nature, a child can choose only a path away from God and what He desires. God has provided parents to guide, teach, train, and restrain; the child left to his own way is unable to do these things himself. NACD believed in providing specific sensory input in a specific manner to train the brain to function in a more orderly way. Sensory integration is crucial for an autistic person, but how it is administered is just as important. Random, chaotic input is useless. Input that is specific and consistent with the appropriate frequency, intensity, and duration is key to having any profitable bearing on the function of the brain.

Although NACD is not a "Christian" organization, nor one that affiliates itself with any particular religion, it does promote certain principles that Christian parents can agree with. We appreciate the fact that NACD did not try to deal with the moral development of our child. We liked the fact that they were experts on the brain. This is what we needed from them. The Scriptures were and are our guide for moral training.

❖ ❖ ❖

We officially started Drew's program on a Monday morning. David and I were prepared to execute this program for the first time ever. We had discussed exactly what and how we were going to do it and even practiced on each other. It was obvious to both of us that we had to be clear and decisive when giving Drew any direction or command. If we showed ourselves the least bit wishy-washy, it would give Drew grounds to oppose us. For everyone's sake, the whole plan had to be perfectly clear in both our minds. Continuity was vital.

"Come here," I said while walking Drew toward me before planting him on the floor in the middle of the living room.

I began to take all but his diaper off and told him exactly what we were going to do.

"Mommy is going to squeeze your arms." I began to apply deep pressure to his arms and hands just as we had watched Cyndi Ringoen show us on the video. Next, I moved to his feet and legs, gently squeezing his limbs.

At first Drew jerked away from all of this "forced touching."

"No, Mommy needs to squeeze your legs," I said, pulling him back gently and holding my ground with all of my confidence. He obeyed.

Next, I put on some special scratchy gloves and began to rub him all over his limbs and chest and back. He let out a loud, disagreeable noise and pulled away. I lessened the pressure and continued.

Each exercise was to last only a few minutes. Eight minutes had passed and we only had twenty-nine more exercises to go. Certainly Drew would scream soon.

The next exercise instructed us to tap lightly or use a feather on his face and neck and head. This was to help lessen his oversensitivity to touch in these areas. Drew freaked out the second I began. It was more than he could bear. He screamed and tried to bury his head between his legs and push away my hands. I looked to David for advice. He nodded at me to continue. Even though we couldn't bear to see Drew so upset, I continued a few more seconds and then I stopped. We figured we needed to at least attempt all of the activities. He would have plenty of time to get used to them.

Next, we had to remember to swirl a toothette (a disposable sponge on the end of a stick) around his mouth. This had to be done four times a day. This was to increase the sensitivity in his mouth which would help later with diction and communication.

David had rigged up the garage as a physical therapy room. We managed to obtain several large refrigerator boxes from a warehouse. David opened them up and laid them on the hard floor of the garage. Drew was to crawl and creep. I didn't realize what a difficult task this would be for him to carry out.

We all got on our hands and knees and began to creep back and forth on all fours. Even though we felt ridiculous participating, we knew it would motivate Drew to do it if we did it with him and kept egging him on.

It was then time to crawl. That meant we had to lie flat on our tummies and perform the "army crawl," extending an arm with an opposite bent leg. This was an exercise in cross-patterning. If a person is unable to do this, it is indicative of a lack of neurological organization in lower parts of the brain. Drew couldn't do it. David showed him how several times, but Drew found it impossible. With David at one end and I at the other, we moved Drew's body through the motions of the cross-patterned crawl. It seemed a very long two minutes, working our way back and forth across the cold cardboard on the floor.

The next activity was to try to get Drew to hop on his right foot. Part of establishing neurological organization is developing dominance of one side of the brain. So the plan was to have Drew develop the left hemisphere of the brain by stimulating the entire right side of his body. Since he showed a natural proclivity to use his right hand, the rest of the body was to follow suit. He was to become not only right-handed, but right-footed, right-eared, and right-eyed. He would wear a patch over his left eye and a plug in his left ear four hours a day to promote the other side becoming the dominant processors of visual and auditory information.

As is common with some autistic children, Drew lacked muscle tone. Along with deep pressure, exercises such as running for ten minutes and sitting and standing from a stool to build tone in his legs were to be done twice a day.

By the time we finished our ten-minute jog, all of us were pooped! We hadn't even gone once through the program. All of the exercises were to be done twice a day, a couple of them four times a day.

I was slowly losing momentum and a positive outlook, as each activity seemed to end up taking much longer than we had planned. Drew continued, though, obediently following through—not always liking it of course, but knowing that Mom and Dad were the boss. Drew would show dislike through whining or crying. David and I just persisted by gently moving him through the motions. Obviously, if he was really upset, we didn't force it for the entire two minutes, or however long it was. The point we were trying to establish was, "This is our new routine. Just do what we say. Just make an attempt . . . that's all we ask." It was good that David and I attempted our first routine together. We quickly tried to work out kinks and make decisions on how best to carry out each task. We also kept each other from giving up.

Before putting a patch on Drew's eye or plugging his ear, we did exercises to strengthen his eyes. Drew had an extreme oversensitivity to light, which led us to conclude that this contributed to his difficulty in making eye contact. We used a small, skinny object like a pencil to practice tracking. A flashlight with a penny taped over the bulb was used to desensitize him to light. Spinning him on a swing in the garage and then abruptly stopping him developed control and strength in the muscles in his eyes. First one way, stop, wait, and then the other way.

I'm sure this whole circus would have seemed abusive to an onlooker that hadn't any idea there was a purpose behind all of this seeming madness. We even laughed a bit to ourselves as we thought of how we looked going through all of these exercises. Oh well, we knew that to help Drew we didn't have to have doctorate degrees, just love and a lot of fortitude. We were positive of the love but, two and a half hours later, we wondered about the fortitude. We were still not even once through the program yet!

We did exercises to strengthen his hands and exercises to strengthen his tongue. We demonstrated math problems and flashed vocabulary words. On and on and still not done yet.

A big part of the program was designed to increase Drew's auditory short-term memory ability. This was accomplished by reciting a string of digits and having Drew say them back to us. To improve visual short-term memory, we showed him several numbers and then removed them from view. Drew then had to repeat what he had seen. This activity was to be done four times a day.

I took a whole bunch of photos of familiar objects throughout the house and even of the places Drew was familiar with, like the store, library, and church. For each photo I showed Drew, I was to say a language-related phrase. For instance, I showed him a picture of his bed and said, "I feel tired." This was to help with language skills.

We were to begin to limit music as much as possible because, we learned, certain specific types of music (especially vocal) stimulate the subdominant part of the brain which is the center of emotions. Until the higher learning part of Drew's brain developed a clear dominance, music only served to stimulate the lower portions of the brain and delay the establishment of dominance. Of everything we did in that first week, it was the virtual elimination of music in our house and in the car that had the most immediate and obvious effect on Drew's behavior. Drew had always listened to the CD player on a daily basis—sometimes for hours if I wasn't reading to him or serving him a meal. He rocked in the rocking chair and became mesmerized with the changing numbers on the player. The day we discontinued "music time" Drew's anxiety level lowered and he seemed to cope better with change throughout the day. He was by no means "cured," but there was a huge improvement in his ability to control his emotions.

Not only was music to be limited, but specific information was to be put in through the auditory channel. David and I made a ten-minute tape of our own voices, skip-counting by 2s, 4s, 5s; we stated general information, such as birthdays, address, and phone number. We also taught him some catechism questions and answers this way. He was to listen with an earphone in his right ear two times a day.

By the time David and I finished the program with Drew, we were all beat. It seemed to consume our whole day. I began to get a sick feeling in my stomach thinking about being all alone the next day when David went to work. In my tired state of mind I started to get panicky. I just couldn't see how I was going to be able to do it.

The next day David left for work and I lay wide awake with nerves, going over the routine of the day in my mind. Yesterday seemed so long ago as I thought of David and me doing all of the exercises together. The only other time I'd remembered having such a desperate feeling and not wanting David to leave me alone was when he returned to work after taking a week off to be with me and our new baby. Drew was such a tiny, helpless life then. David and I had muddled through our first week of parenthood, struggling with the strangeness of a diaper and figuring out formula measurements together. I couldn't imagine doing all that by myself . . . but somehow I did. Now here I was again, just four years later with the same feelings of anxiety and incompetence I felt as a new mother. Just as Drew's personal well-being was completely my responsibility then, here it was again—only this time the issues were so much bigger. I was now not only responsible for making sure Drew was fed and clean and cared for, but now his whole future was staring me in the face. The weight of that responsibility and dependency on me was overwhelming.

Unable to let myself lie in bed any longer, I got up and took a bath and got ready for the day. After feeding the boys and settling Elliot in the playpen for a play period, I went and got Drew.

"Come here and sit down," I motioned to the spot on the floor in front of me.

Drew obeyed and we began our sensory session again. Drew had the same reaction as the previous day when it came to lightly touching his face and head. I cut the time short after making a definite effort. We continued to progress through the program at nearly the same pace and success as the day before, only this time without David's moral and physical support to keep me going.

I tried to spend short, planned times with Elliot throughout the day so that he wouldn't feel left out. When I put Elliot down for his nap in the afternoon, I took Drew out to the garage for his physical exercise. We began with creeping for two minutes on all fours.

"C'mon, sweetie—keep going. Just follow Mommy. That's right."

Drew was cooperating so much better than I had counted on. He almost seemed to like the full schedule the day provided. Each time we changed activities he would try to oppose me as he usually did when it came to change, but I always stuck to my guns and never gave in. I knew that all could be easily lost if I faltered even once. I just couldn't afford to let Drew win even one battle...and he couldn't afford it either.

I was beginning to feel tired by this point in the day and my initial nervous momentum that got me through the first part of the day had just oozed out. As I knelt behind Drew on the hard cardboard floor, trying to put his body through the motions of the cross-pattern army crawl, I started to lose it. Drew just didn't get what I was trying to do with him. He wasn't rebelling, but he wasn't doing it right either. Without warning I heard terrible words come shooting out of my mouth at Drew's back as he lay on his tummy before me.

"Not like that," I yelled. "Move this arm back when this leg is here."

I jerked his body into position.

Drew started to cry, burying his face in the cardboard.

"Oh, honey," I gasped, "Mommy was wrong. I'm so sorry. Please, please forgive me." I lay on the cardboard next to him—so afraid to touch him, knowing how he despised affection. I wanted with all my heart to enfold him in my arms and rock him tenderly against me. But all I could do was lie next to him and weep.

After a brief moment we stopped and I just looked at the back of his head as he lay only inches from me physically, but turned completely from me emotionally. My hair stuck to my face. I felt drained and lifeless. There was just no way this little lost boy could understand the importance of all this to him. He lived in the here and now—con-

156

stantly struggling to make meaning of events as they happened to him. I suddenly felt a sense of complete helplessness. It was impossible to save his life. All I could do was try to help him, but I couldn't save him, no matter how hard I tried.

We finished in silence, going through the motions of our activities. I was exhausted by the end of the day and there were still records to keep and paperwork to complete. When David came home from work, he found me with my head resting on my arms on the kitchen table. Paperwork and vocabulary cards and digit cards lay scattered around me.

"Honey—are you okay?" came the tender voice.

"I can't do it . . . I just can't maintain this pace," I whispered without lifting my head.

David's strong arms came around me. I began to cry. I felt defeated and that I somehow had betrayed my son. *If I really loved him, I could do it all for him,* I thought. *I'm a failure.*

Later in bed that night we talked about what to do. In the dark, I felt the care in David's voice. "It won't help anybody if this is just too much for you to take on."

He was right. I had two children that needed me. I had always had an "all or nothing" mentality. Objective David soothed my mind with words of common sense. He was right. How could I possibly measure my love for Drew by how many check marks I was able to put on a piece of paper?

"All you can do is all you can do," he whispered to me.

I fell fast asleep, content that the decision to accomplish only what I could the next day was a wise and profitable goal. And that's what I did.

It took a couple of weeks to develop a routine that seemed balanced, and it didn't take Drew long to come to anticipate the next exercise of the day. Our days were full, with an exercise always needing to be done. The program was to be carried out seven days a week. David and I didn't prefer being so busy on the Lord's Day, because it was our conviction that it was to be a day of rest, devoted to the worship of God. We wrestled with what to do about the program for that day. After much thought and prayer, we decided to do what we could because the program, to us, was like Drew's medicine. We reasoned that we wouldn't deny David's dad his blood pressure medication for a day, if that's what his body needed; neither could we deny Drew what his brain needed to improve. The key to the program was the frequency and the duration of each activity. This repetitive and consistently applied stimulation was training the brain to function more and more normally. He needed every dose he could get.

One evening two weeks into our new lifestyle, I sat propped up on the couch, finishing up my daily records of Drew's progress. Elliot was babbling happily on the kitchen floor next to David's feet while David helped Drew with a drink of water from a glass. Suddenly, a crash startled me as the glass accidentally slipped from Drew's hands and fell against the hard kitchen sink. Before I could think or get up, I saw Drew's frightened face headed straight for me. It all happened so fast. The next thing I felt was my boy's tense little body pushing against mine. *Yes. I do believe it is . . .* I thought to myself. I stared down at Drew's body buried into my lap, his arms awkwardly wrapped around my hips. A hug. The very first he'd ever given me. I didn't know what to do. If I reciprocated, the blessedness might end and maybe never happen again. But I couldn't help myself and risked it anyway. Gently placing my arms around him, I closed my eyes and hugged him back. Time stood still. And then it was over. Just as fast as it had happened, it was all over. Drew sped away to isolate himself in his room.

"David! David! Did you see that?" I yelled, scattering my papers as I ran to the kitchen where David was busy cleaning up broken glass. "Drew hugged me . . . he really hugged me!"

David's eyes welled up with tears at the news. We simply looked at each other and smiled. There was no need for words as we embraced each other. Our Drew had spoken, and louder than ever.

❖ ❖ ❖

With each day that passed, our routine became more sure. That isolated display of affection motivated us to press on. And there were other subtle changes happening as well. We detected a slight improvement in eye contact and a little more relaxed demeanor.

Four weeks into the program, we attended a previously scheduled speech therapy appointment with Bier. It was to be our last.

I was a little nervous as we approached her office after parking the car. Would this critic of what we are doing with our son notice any improvement in Drew? David opened the door to the waiting room so that Drew and I could enter. It was unusual to see another family sitting in the tiny room. A couple in their forties sat in chairs and didn't look up from their books when we entered. A boy a bit older than Drew was roughly playing with some of the available toys. After spotting us, he came over to me with a toy in his hands and let out a yell. It was obvious he wanted my attention but didn't know exactly how to get it. The parents continued reading. I glanced down at Drew who was watching this loud, bustling child with a look of awe mixed with fear. Bier suddenly rounded the corner and looked concerned when she saw me.

"Oh, I thought we scheduled your appointment for an hour from now. There seems to be a mix up," she finished, looking at her wristwatch for verification.

"That's fine," I said. "We can come back in an hour. I'm terribly sorry."

As we were about to turn to go, an eruption took place from the waiting party. Bier looked at the boy and said, "Okay, Brian, let's go play. C'mon back with Bier." She stretched out her hand toward the boy who instantly began to scream.

"No! No! No!"

This vocalization seemed to finally rouse the parents from their novels momentarily.

Bier spoke to the air rather than to anyone in particular. "Maybe

Mom or Dad could bring you back." She turned to go to one of the therapy rooms. With this subtle directive, the mother rose.

"Let's go, Brian. Now c'mon."

Brian's opposition increased in volume and intensity as he pushed with all of his might against his mother's body.

I again looked down at Drew. I had never seen him so enthralled with other people. He watched the struggling mother and son with arms limp at his sides and mouth slightly agape. I was surprised. Not wanting Drew to learn any more from Brian, David and I whisked him out of the room where Brian's wails could still be heard through the closed door behind us. Finally, back in the car, David looked at me with a sarcastic glance back toward the building before pulling out of the parking lot to kill some time. When we arrived back at the office an hour later, there was no sign of Brian or his parents.

Bier greeted us in the now quiet waiting room. I was so full of questions, I could hardly contain myself.

"How old was that little boy? Is he autistic? Do you know if he is receiving any other kinds of therapy?" I was still very curious to see how Drew compared to others with the same disabilities.

Bier answered and actually seemed very proud of Brian and his accomplishments. He had been coming to her for several years as well as attending the public school's special education class. He was only a year and a half older than Drew. Bier said that Brian and Drew had very similar problems with language and processing.

Bier then turned to greet Drew. Drew naturally turned away, but David turned him back toward Bier and said, "Say, 'Hello, Mrs. Bier.'" Drew obeyed and then we followed her back to one of the rooms. Almost immediately, Bier commented on Drew. "He really seems more relaxed," she said, studying him.

I couldn't help myself and blurted, "Do you really think so?"

"Oh yes, he seems very different," she said, not taking her eyes off him. "Have you started that program you told me about?"

"Yes, and it's going great!"

160

I told her about it and about "The Hug." Bier listened with interest. "Well, whatever you are doing, it seems to be helping," she said, smiling at me.

After working with Drew for a while she repeated her positive words about him. I was elated the whole rest of the day. Her words meant a lot, since she hadn't actually thought that NACD was the best route to take; but she couldn't deny that there was noticeable, even if slight, improvement in Drew after only one month.

That night while David dressed Drew for bed, I heard, from the living room, an unusual dialogue between them.

"C'mon, Drew, let's put your pajamas on now."

"No, no, no," came the steady but quiet reply.

Drew had never in his life told one of us "no." I was shocked as I waited to hear what David would do.

"We do not say no to Mommy or Daddy. That little boy was wrong to say that to his Mommy," David said in his most serious-sounding voice.

Apparently, Drew obeyed without an incident because he appeared with his pajamas on a few minutes later. I was glad that it was over and now could be forgotten.

The following day we proceeded with our exercises as usual. When we were about halfway through, I was shocked to hear it again.

"No, no, no," said Drew quietly in response to my requiring we complete the exercise we were on.

Knowing that David had just dealt with him the day before, I corrected him immediately. "We do not tell Mommy or Daddy no. You need to obey and say, 'Yes, Mommy.' I put him on his bed to settle down. I needed to settle down, too. I was sorry that Drew had had to witness Brian's rebellion and his parents' lack of control or authority over him. I became increasingly upset when I thought of the fact that Brian was just one of the many peers Drew would have had if we had put him in the special ed. preschool class as we had been directed. Is

161

screaming and yelling "no" at a mother or father when you don't want to do something an "autistic symptom," or is it rebellion that needs to be dealt with? Would Drew's socialization abilities improve from being around other "Brians," or would that kind of exposure quickly chisel away at what David and I had already tried to teach him about socialization? The socialization skills we had tried to instill in Drew had been those of self-control, patience, kindness, sharing, being polite, waiting your turn, obeying authority figures, greeting someone who greets you, helping others, being tidy, and so on. Aren't these the qualities that make someone a socially acceptable person? I was becoming even more convinced that what we were doing at home with Drew was the very best thing for him.

Drew quickly settled himself and I went in and put my arms around him. He sat stiff on his bed but allowed me to hug him. He didn't pull away. "I love you, honey . . . everything is okay."

We went on to finish our exercises for the day and Drew never told us no again.

❖ ❖ ❖

Two months into the program, Drew became officially and completely potty trained. He was four years, four months old, and I was more than ready to be through with diapers. It was a day of rejoicing.

As Drew's auditory short-term memory improved, his improving language resulted in behaviors and anxieties gradually diminishing. We could see a glimmer of understanding in his eyes as he was finally learning, ever so slightly, the meaning and purpose of the use of language. This step helped in the area of potty training. Although for months we had told him that he needed to come to us and tell us he had to go before he went in his pants, it never seemed to make sense to him what all of the babble was about. Then one day it happened. A panicked-looking Drew rounded the corner of the kitchen where I was working and shrieked while clutching the front of his pants, "If you have to go potty, you need to say, 'I want to go potty please!' "

Finally, he was beginning to see that certain words could be associated with certain activities and actually convey a need. We raced together to the bathroom where all of the liquid went into the desired destination.

"Hurray, you did it. You told Mommy you needed to go potty. Good job, Drew!"

I actually heard a slight chuckle of satisfaction come from him as he finished up. He understood. He could learn. He never went in his pants again.

18
Yet Am I Not Forsaken

David and I decided to stop seeing Bier. We didn't see how a once-a-month "play time" with her was all that important to Drew's improvement. Drew was getting very specific and consistent therapy from us every day that was proving to do more for him than speech drills and games. I was understanding more clearly the importance of attacking the problem at its source. Ultimately, Drew's problem was not a behavior problem; therefore, behavior modification was not the best solution because his behaviors were only symptoms. Drew's problem wasn't ultimately a speech problem either; therefore, speech therapy wasn't entirely the answer. Drew's brain was unorganized, and because of sensory and auditory and visual sequential processing problems, certain symptoms showed themselves; but it was his brain that needed retraining. Then the other areas of concern would naturally take care of themselves.

I envisioned the brain as a house, with many ways of gaining access to it. There are windows, doors, mail drop, chimney, etc. By using behavior modification drills or repetitious speech games, we would see, over time, improvement in Drew. We would slowly gain access through the door of Drew's mind. Using the other therapies we learned about would be like bringing all of the groceries into the house through the mail drop alone because we would be dealing only with the *symptoms* of autism. This would eventually get the groceries into the house, but why not just fix the hinges of the entire door so that access would be more natural and efficient? Drew's brain was our target. We viewed our daily exercises of physical activity, sequential processing, establishing dominance in his brain, and sensory integration as oiling the hinges and replacing a faulty doorknob. Access was becoming available and Drew was beginning to improve.

Another element was added to Drew's program which helped to

establish neurological organization and desensitize his hearing: developmental auditory training. Through NACD, we began a home sound therapy program. Specially designed CDs would send out frequencies to help desensitize Drew's oversensitive hearing and help promote his auditory processing skills. They were to be listened to through specified headphones that helped to block out noises in the environment.

Since Drew loved the CD player already, this addition was more of a treat than a burden. After one month of listening daily, I recorded this information:

> Although it is hard for us to see any real difference in
> Drew, his Sunday School teacher, who sees him once a
> week, has made some comments we feel are worth noting.
> She mentioned that in the last few weeks he really seems
> to be paying more attention and has better eye contact.
> He also has not shown as much anxiety over disruptions in
> the routine if they should happen to occur. The teacher
> even commented that he tried to make a joke with her
> and had found something really silly. Until now, he hasn't
> really shown an appropriate sense of humor.

It was about this time that Drew had his first re-evaluation with Cyndi since beginning the program. She noted an improvement in him right away and commented that his auditory digit span had jumped from four digits to five. This was a significant improvement. Drew now had the ability to cross-pattern crawl, which completed the organization of the lower level brain functions—the foundation on which all higher levels of organization are built. If we hadn't understood the relationship between his brain and being able to cross-pattern crawl, we wouldn't have recognized the significance of this feat.

Two more months into auditory training, I wrote these notes:

> I have noticed an improvement in language. He's using

it correctly and using it more! He has even attempted correcting himself in using the proper pronoun. I've noticed an increase in imaginary play and in understanding humor. He laughs appropriately and we've even shared in many laughs together. It's like he "gets it." Anxiety and opposition have decreased and he seems increasingly able to regain his composure more quickly. I've noticed that it doesn't disturb him when I sing anymore. He used to get very bothered if I should start singing—even from the other room. I've even heard him humming to himself a couple of times. He had never done that.

With each evaluation that followed that first year, Drew showed dramatic improvement. We were continuing to carry out the program every day and making adjustments each time we received the new program in the mail. The auditory training continued as well, every day for the first year. Cyndi told us with enthusiasm that Drew was the fastest improving autistic child she had ever worked with. She attributed the speed of his improvement to the fact that we were not distracted by trying to control his behavior. Drew was not exempt from learning what obedience was, and God honored this. Since he was able to obey, the foundation to treating him was laid.

These notes were taken after the next evaluation:

Drew was seen by Cyndi on June 8, 1997. She commented on how much more aware he seemed. His comprehension was greatly improved. At the previous evaluation in January, Cyndi was unable to even test for reading comprehension. On June 8, Drew tested at a second grade, ninth month for reading comprehension. He seems to be using language more and better. Has been asking more "wh" questions*. (Although still not a "why" question)

One month later:

Drew continues to improve in language. He corrects himself more on his pronoun reversals. He seems more relaxed and laughs frequently and appropriately. He seems much more social and actually appears to love playing and laughing with his brother now. He used to prefer being more isolated and spend his time on his computer rather than interact with his brother. He seems able to get self-control much more quickly if upset about something.

I was standing in the kitchen fixing lunch one afternoon. The squeals of laughter coming from Drew and Elliot as they played together down the hallway were music to my ears. How I had longed for this brother-with-brother play. Being so young, Elliot had never suspected anything was wrong with his big brother. He had only admired him and waited for his friendship . . . and now it was here.

Suddenly something Drew did made me stop my sandwich making and thank God. I had never heard Drew talk the way he did that instant, and it made me smile to myself.

"No, Elliot. Move over!" yelled Drew.

Normally, talking this way to someone would be corrected, but the thought that hit me was, Drew now saw himself as an individual. He was fighting for his rights to some space. What a remarkable revelation for him. He was a person and he was using his words to convey meaning to another person. What a beautiful thing.

*What, where, when, why

167

19
Sweet Comfort Yet Shall Fill My Heart

It was going to happen on October 10, 1997. I could hardly wait. I was actually going to meet her and hear her speak—the woman who first introduced us to the monster and set us on this journey, Temple Grandin. It had been over a year since David and I saw her featured on TV, promoting her book and talking about her life with autism. She had not a clue I even existed, but that didn't matter. I felt as though I knew her personally and intimately now after a year of living with and trying to understand this horrible thing called autism.

Mixed with my excitement was a growing fear as I rode with a friend up to Seattle where the autism conference was being held. My stomach was in a knot and I could feel a lump in my throat. In my mind the dank and rainy morning seemed to be holding us still and keeping us from getting there any faster than a crawl. When we finally did pull into the parking lot of the hotel, I was happy to see that we were early, which meant that we had a chance at some good seats. My friend and I raced to the building, shielding our faces with our umbrellas from the rainy wind. We found the conference room and quickly signed in at the door. The huge room was dimly lit and filled with long tables covered with linen and dotted with water glasses. We found some seats right in front of the podium. I couldn't have been happier. I hadn't waited this long for this event to have to struggle to see her. I wanted to absorb her every move and gesture.

I was beginning to understand my feelings as I sat motionless before the empty podium. Why should I feel so connected to a complete stranger? I was acting like I was going to meet a long lost child! That was it. Temple represented Drew, only Drew all grown up. It was my own special glimpse into the future. Temple was fifty years old, but she and Drew had scored exactly the same on Rimland's E2 checklist.

Whatever she was like was what Drew would be like in forty-five years.

"That's her," my friend whispered to me, sending my attention to the back of the room.

My eyes were glued on her as I felt a rush of emotion nearly come spilling out. There sat a grown woman who appeared normal enough to me, organizing some slides she needed for her presentation. She was alone.

"Go on and meet her," my friend encouraged me, knowing that my chances would soon grow limited the more time went by and the more people arrived. We got up and moved to where she was sitting, my eyes never leaving her. The nearer we got to her the more frightened I felt. My breathing became fast and my hands got hot and sweaty. What would I say? *I can't do this!* All I could do was stare and walk just inches past her and then on to the book table set up in the back of the room. I turned and stared at her back. I couldn't speak and I was frustrated that I was feeling so emotional. I felt I would begin sobbing at any minute. I found my way back to my seat defeated. People were really starting to pour in now and I didn't want to lose my spot. I missed my opportunity. What was I so afraid of? Maybe a peek at the future was too daunting for me!

After everyone had gathered and found a place, it was time to begin. Temple approached the podium wearing black jeans and boots and a western-style shirt. She wore no makeup and simply brushed her short hair back from her long face. Once she began speaking, I felt myself calm down. She was the same as when we saw her on TV just a year before. She came across as intelligent and articulate, and when she spoke she reminded me very much of an enthusiastic twelve-year-old boy exhibiting a love for a science project.

The issues she stressed, among other things, as crucial to think about when working with autistic children, were structure and an environment free of sensory overstimulation. She also mentioned the benefits of one-on-one early intervention and constant interaction; the

169

need for concrete examples of good and bad behavior; the need for rules to learn and to guide behavior; the emphatic need of limits upon the autistic; and, finally, that good parenting is the best early intervention. Out of all of the experts on the panel that day, Temple, the autistic, made the most sense to me.

A week before I saw Temple, Drew began displaying appropriate pronoun usage. It was a major breakthrough. It had seemed that we'd been constantly correcting him for years and not giving in until he said it right. Finally, with this language glitch corrected, all of our lives were instantly more relaxed.

November was the final evaluation for our first year with NACD. Having just turned five years old that August, Drew did remarkably well. He scored at a fifth grade level in reading, a third grade level in reading comprehension, and a second grade, ninth month, in math skills. His auditory and visual digit spans tested at six to seven digits. Cyndi commented on how much he interacted with her and just how much more "normal" he seemed. The biggest improvement this time was in the area of socialization and a not-so-anxious demeanor.

Drew's fifth birthday was the first birthday during which he was really "with" us, in the sense of his awareness of what was going on around him and the purpose of the gifts. He showed a happy face as he blew out the candles and a healthy anticipation as he ripped open his presents. He impressed his grandma by reading the birthday card she had given him, out loud. His favorite gifts were some preschool activity books in which he was to color and match and add stickers of shapes and objects in the appropriate spots. While doing dishes one afternoon, I had to suppress a giggle as I heard Drew reading the directions at the bottom of the page of one of his activity books:

"Parents: Have child match the shapes on the left with the shapes on the right," he read with perfect accuracy and then began to match.

After working with NACD for a year and attending the conference with Temple, I knew Drew wouldn't be considered perfectly normal yet, although he was much more of a joy to live with.

One thing we all enjoyed doing as a family was eating out at a Japanese restaurant. Both children just loved the teriyaki chicken, and we rarely had to take home leftovers. After finishing up my last bite of chicken and rice one evening, I leaned back in my chair and sighed, "Mommy is going to pop."

From the look of confusion on Drew's face, I could tell that I still needed to be careful of what I said around my hyper-literalist son. He stopped mid-chew and gave me a blank look. I could tell he was trying to envision how it would look for Mommy to do such a thing. I quickly corrected my statement and knew that whatever I said satisfied him, because he began to chew again.

At the end of the meal, we received our check and a fortune cookie for each of us. Drew was thrilled to read our messages to all of us. When he got to mine, I couldn't help thinking of the irony of what it said. He read slowly but distinctly, "Someone you want to reach could be mysteriously away." If he only knew how this "someone," who had been mysteriously away, was away no longer. He was so close that we could now reach him, and we would never, never let him go.

20
And So to Him I Leave It All

The ugliest thing about autism is that you can't see its source. Tucked away and hidden behind a perfectly normal looking face is an injured brain. Injured so horribly it produces only what it can: bizarre and confusing behavior. How much easier autism would be to accept and understand if we could see past the noise and chaos of the strange behavior to what is really at the core of the problem: the brain. If Drew had been born with a deformed and twisted leg, we would not marvel at his limp. Without a doubt, autistic behavior is misunderstood and frightening, so misunderstood that people have gone to great extremes to try to explain it. Until a more objective standard of diagnosis is used and the cause of autism is determined, the confusion and theories will be perpetuated.

As Christian parents we have a duty before God and a responsibility to the children He has given us. We must consider all in this life from a theological perspective. We must remind ourselves, in times of confusion and of doubt, of what we know to be true based on the Scriptures alone, and then act accordingly.

- Nothing occurs outside the will of the sovereign God of the universe.
- God is holy and wise.
- All things are for our growth in sanctification.
- God may or may not heal, but still we are commanded to pray.
- God is able to heal, and will, according to His good pleasure.
- Our children have been created in the image of God and are moral creatures.
- Autistic or not, our children must be raised in the fear and admonition of the Lord.

172

- Decisions made in life about how to approach specific circumstances must be rationally disciplined by the principles laid out in Scripture.

This list of reminders is a smattering of truths to cling to when tossed by grief, or worry, or indecision. I would never say that a certain method or therapy is the "Biblical" one or isn't, but I can say the method of parenting or treatment of autism springs forth from someone's philosophy and worldview. There aren't Biblical "methods," i.e., parenting, education, and treatment approaches, but rather Biblical "principles." Methods stem from principles, and principles define one's philosophy or worldview. Understanding this should help stabilize you, should you ever meet with the torrent of grief and confusion that a diagnosis of autism brings.

I sit at my desk gazing out at our yard, reveling in the beauty of the evening sun sending its light across the grass. The laughter of children's voices mixes with the sound of the garden rake scraping against the cold cement of the driveway. Drew is a couple of months past his fifth birthday and enjoying his play outside in the cool November air. His brother Elliot is doing his best to keep up as he helps his daddy with the task of gathering the autumn leaves into a huge, colorful pile. The intense, frequent screams and constant anxiety which characterized Drew only a year before are gone. The complete inability to communicate with words or to show any affection is descriptive of another boy who lived with us a long, long time ago. This past year has marked the slow death of the monster that never slept. Today, as I hear Drew's easy laughter and catch a glimpse of the sleeve of his jacket as he runs by, I no longer feel the dominance of that monster. I no longer fear it, and I no longer grieve for the son it afflicted.

With Drew's emergence into our world has come my own emergence from the dreadful pit of despair. There are still areas in which to improve, of course; there may always be. But I know that normalcy now outweighs oddity; and Drew's personality shines brighter than the glare that ever came from that horrid monster. By the grace of God, we have hope for the future.

Our God is truly "too wise to be mistaken" and yes, oh yes, "too good to be unkind."

Conclusion

My objective in writing this book is not necessarily to promote a certain program or therapy as much as it is to encourage Christian parents to think Biblically. By this I mean starting where the Scriptures start: the nature of God and the nature of man. God is holy and sovereign; man is fallen and self-consumed. Ultimately, how you view these two things will affect everything you do in life. It will define your worldview. The training of Drew's conscience did not cure him from autism, but it prepared the way for us to help him. Looking back, we can only surmise how easily things could have turned out differently. If David and I had followed the humanistic parenting philosophies of our day and catered to his every whim, concerning ourselves more with his emotions and psyche, we are positive Drew would have become completely out of control, without any hope of being reeled back in. It's not that we didn't care about his emotions, but we needed to see his emotions within the context of his nature. His heart was our focus and will continue to be.

Our early efforts to work on his character by structuring his day was a crucial factor in Drew's recovery from autism. It has been shown that the best treatment plan for autistic children is a highly structured, one-on-one environment. From day one, Drew has had that. Although initially the routine was being utilized to accomplish another objective in Drew's life, it turned out to be the thing his brain most needed to survive and prevent it from regressing even more.

The crucial factor in Drew's improvement came from the fundamental lesson learned through the use of a routine, that being, learning to submit and take direction from us. Without this vital lesson, we would not have been able to utilize the exercises from NACD as efficiently. Our struggle would have instead centered around his lack of compliance rather than on the actual exercises to help his brain

175

improve the way it functioned.

I have come to believe that self-stimulatory behavior* is like a drug the autistic person resorts to when he becomes overwhelmed with his environment. The more he uses it, the more he needs it to survive. By limiting the use of these coping behaviors and gently weaning the "addict," you will help him to deal with the world around him and he will learn to need them less and less. This weaning process happens best in an extremely limited and predictable environment which must be created by the parents.

Since behavior stems not only from the head but also from the heart, we could never be positive that Drew's seeming non-compliant behaviors were exclusively a result of autism or of rebellion. Perhaps it was a little of both. Who could know? This is why we could not exempt him from obedience. By training him in obedience, we could be positive we were consistently addressing the issues of his heart. Coupling this with our consistent training of his brain, we were sure to cover all the bases for both his physical *and* moral development.

Below is a list of practical helps to remember when working with your very special child:

1. Parents don't cause their child to be autistic, but they are integral to the promotion or restraint of its symptoms.
2. Consistency, consistency, consistency. It is important not to confuse consistency with severity. Become keen on recognizing what is too much for your child and finding an appropriate balance based on his abilities and maturity.
3. Develop a predictable routine and an orderly environment.
4. Approach him or her face-to-face: quietly, clearly, simply, and visually.
5. Never forget that your child is a moral being, and never forget

---

* "Sensory play," "stimming," "self-stimulating behaviors" all refer to activities which stimulate the senses of the person doing them.

your responsibility to train his conscience.

6. He is not exempt from learning to obey the first time he is told. But at the same time, consider how easily he can become confused whenever you approach him. Don't spring things on him and always help him prepare.

7. Whether or not you can determine the problem that is setting him off at the moment, never let him think that losing control is acceptable.

8. Never give in to outbursts. Respond exactly the same way (words and consequences) at each offense. Remember, he learns according to pattern.

9. It is said by some that you cannot discipline autistic children because they do not understand the concept of cause and effect. This concept, just as the concepts of language and every other concept we strive to teach them to survive in this world, can be *taught*.*

10. Stress encouragement. Look for opportunities to offer positive feedback.

11. Limit the variables in his life to make everything as predictable as possible.

12. Rather than falling into the trap of responding to his outbursts, *prevent* them by doing all you can to order his day. Make him comply to your ways, not the other way around.

13. Limit free time as much as possible and engage him in as much one-on-one human contact as you can.

14. Remember that the less chaos in his environment, the more learning can take place.

15. Flexibility can and should be taught, but only after a solid pat-

---

* According to attorney Scott Somerville, noted authority on parental rights, "Every state prohibits *injuring* a child, but permits parents to use reasonable corporal discipline in the best interest of the child. A small but effective 'sting' is much safer for the autistic child than the consequences of his or her own uncontrolled behavior."

tern has been established and then only in small increments according to his ability to tolerate it.

16. Nothing can do more damage than a husband and a wife who don't agree on an approach.

17. Some behavior problems can easily and quickly be eliminated by adjusting the child's diet and eliminating foods which may be causing an allergic response.

18. Make his world very small, help him cope there, and slowly open it up for him. You will know that your child is able to handle more freedom when he is able to cope well in the smallness of the world you created for him.

19. By simply trying to deal with behavior problems and not with the root problems of sensory processing, you will accomplish very little and most likely exasperate your child and yourself.

20. Do all you can to accommodate the child's frame, whether by way of diet, routine, and/or sensory perception considerations, and then set a moral standard and stick to it.

May God bless you in your quest to recover your child.

Afterword

I met the Steeres in late 1996. I remember asking to take Drew into another room with me by himself to do some of the testing. His mother was obviously anxious about this, but gave permission. Drew did well on the testing and tried hard to do everything I asked of him. It was apparent from the evaluation that Drew had serious problems in being overly sensitive to many things, including surface touch, light, and sound, to name a few; and at the same time he was undersensitive to deep pressure. Because of this his entire gross motor and vestibular processes were greatly impaired. But when his parents were present, I was greatly impressed by Drew's obvious attempts at trying to maintain his behavior even when frightened by new sounds; e.g., the heater coming on. I remember commenting to the Steeres that it was obvious someone had spent a lot of time working with him on discipline because I had never met a child as sensitive as Drew who also had the ability to try to control his responses while dealing with uncomfortable and frightening stimuli. It was also clear that someone had spent a lot of time reading with Drew, as his reading level was high first grade and he was only four years old.

As the Steeres left to begin their journey with a program outlined specifically for Drew, I worried about how they would fare. The family had a lot of assets: a very structured, energetic mom who was impatient for progress, but patient with Drew—Drew, who was obviously tremendously intelligent and disciplined enough to receive instruction—and a father who was incredibly involved with his family and their well being. I was hoping that I could count on David to be the voice of reason, moderation and support for Cathy as they embarked on this journey.

I am sure that the first four months of the program were probably by far their most difficult. Trying to find the balance between wanting to do each activity perfectly and exactly, with the reality of having another small child to care for and a limited amount of energy. Despite the struggle, they made terrific progress, and when they came for the first reevaluation, Drew had improved in reading by several years, math by one year; his sensitivities were decreasing, his gross motor skills were coming together, his short-term memory had improved by over a year, and he was potty trained.

Drew has continued over the last two years to make great and steady progress. Much of the credit goes to his mother who has been consistent and willing to sacrifice her time for Drew. Maybe even more credit goes to Drew's father who continually provides moral support, strength, and the ever-needed voice of moderation to his wife. But I believe that most of the progress was obtained so quickly because of Cathy and David's conviction about their responsibility to raise a moral child. Because of this, they spent many years, before I ever met them, instilling in Drew the need for following direction and being obedient. This was the most important foundation they could have possibly laid for him. It wasn't until he was four years old that they found the answer to help Drew overcome his autistic symptoms, but because of the foundation, they could then take the answer and run with it—getting immediate and dramatic results in the process.

I have met hundreds, maybe thousands, of parents over the last decade who were looking for answers and struggling with children who have been diagnosed with various conditions. Nothing is sadder than when they are given the answers but cannot proceed past that point because the child's behavior will not allow it. In the worst case, the parents give up because the struggle with the child is too intense. In other cases, the progress continues, but at a much slower rate because the child's behavior constantly interferes with it. Having the privilege to work with families such as the Steeres constantly reinforces my faith that God's way works under any and all circumstances. And that by following God's commands with faith—even when it seems fruitless—will bring you rewards that you could never anticipate.

Because of David and Cathy's faith and obedience to God under the most trying of circumstances, they have been able in two and a half years to help Drew progress at an incredible speed. Drew at age six and a half years can read at ninth grade level, comprehend at fourth grade level, do math at fourth grade level. His gross motor skills have improved and he can now run, jump, kick, skip, etc. His short-term memory skills are superior to most adults, his hypersensitivities are gone. He has conversational language and even jokes.

I would like to commend Cathy for her courage in providing such an open and honest account of her family's pain, struggle, and triumph through this confusing mystery of autism.

Cyndi Ringoen, B.A., B.S., NeuroDevelopmentalist

Excerpts from the

Journal of the National Academy for Child Development

1986 Volume 6, No. 11

The Autistic Child
by Robert J. Doman, Jr.

Children labeled as "autistic" have been enigmas since they were first identified. Fortunately, some questions surrounding these children are being answered. Many "autistic" children (children with sensory dysfunction) are now being helped, and some are achieving "normal" function. As a result of NACD's work with "autistic" children, we have also gained a better understanding of sensory function. This understanding has had implications and applications to our work with all children.

Historically, the parents of "autistic" children have suffered more (if such suffering can in fact be measured) than the parents of any other group of children. The classic "autistic" child was viewed as a child with a severe emotional problem, or as a child with childhood schizophrenia. Often, this emotional or psychiatric condition was attributed to maternal rejection. In addition to society's punishment of the parent (particularly of the mother for supposedly rejecting her child), was the child's behavior, which often appeared to others as rejection of people in general, and to the mother as a rejection of her in particular. Add to this the child's often rather bizarre, and in some cases, destructive behavior, and you have a description of a very untenable situation. Such is one's introduction to the world of the "autistic" child. Fortunately, as with many of the mystiques built up around unanswered questions, the view of the "autistic" child as an emotionally disturbed child is based upon supposition, not fact. Suppositions that we strongly question.

The Isolated "Autistic" Child

Generally, descriptions of "autistic" children are rather similar. They are essentially descriptions of symptoms, leaving the questions of cause and cure open.

When Fenichel (1960) described children with "childhood schizophrenia" he described the "autistic" child as follows: "They have little or no speech, they rarely display any effective awareness of people, and they maintain a level of activity that has the barest relation to objects or events in the real world." Fenichel then subdivides "autistic" children into two groups: "those who have been retarded in maturation from birth, and those children with a history of regression."

Kanner, in 1958, established criteria for infantile autism as the following: "An extreme self-isolation, or an inability to relate themselves in the ordinary way to people or situations from early in life," and "an obsessive insistence of the maintenance of sameness."

Children who have been diagnosed as "autistic" function within a very broad range. On the mild end of the spectrum are children who in many ways look and even act rather "normal," but who may have some perseverative or repetitive behaviors such as rocking, humming, or repeating verbatim what is said to them (echolalia). At the other extreme are children whose behavior appears to fit many people's perception of a severely emotionally disturbed individual. Such children are characterized by behavior that can be very hyper (active) or hypo (inactive); they can be destructive, self-destructive, and at times aggressive. All such children can generally be described as exhibiting some degree of self-isolation.

A Problem of Perception

The "autistic" child can be perceived as an emotionally disturbed child without a great deal of difficulty. They are often in their own little world, and they essentially do reject others to varying degrees. They may strike out at others, at their environment, and even at themselves as though consumed by some inner emotional force. But if we view these behaviors through other eyes, they can begin to make even greater sense.

Why do many "autistic" children have perfectly "normal" siblings? Why do many "autistic" children have warm, loving mothers? Why do some children begin life "normally" and regress into an "autistic" condition a year, or two, or three after birth? These questions cannot be easily answered with the "emotional" model; however, they can be answered with the "neurological/sensory" model. . . .

NACD's perception of the "autistic" child follows the neurological/sensory model. A child who has been labeled as "autistic" is viewed not as an emotionally disturbed child, or as a child with a psychiatric problem, but as a child with sensory dysfunction whose abnormal behavior is a reflection of abnormal perception.

Typically, a child given an emotional/psychiatric label is not examined or evaluated beyond the parameters of the problem as it is perceived. However, NACD has had the opportunity to examine the results of full neurological workups of "autistic" children. The results of such workups indicate that "autistic" children are brain-injured. . . .

Sensory Dysfunction

NACD refers to the "autistic" child as a child with sensory dysfunction. Our work with these children begins by evaluating function in order to determine the degree and type of abnormal sensory function. That is to say, by looking at how the child reacts, it is possible to make a determination as to how the child perceives the world, which then makes it possible to assess the child's problems in the various sensory channels. How we see the world is determined by how our brains interpret the information that comes through our five senses. . . . The way we see the world is determined by how our brains interpret it. . . . Each child needs to be considered on an individual basis. Evaluation of an individual is complicated by the interaction of the five sensory channels.

Emergence of a Pattern

Through our work with children who have sensory dysfunction, a pattern has emerged into which more than half of the "autistic" children appear to fit. This pattern includes the following: hyper-auditory, hypo-central vision, hyper-peripheral vision, hyper-touch, hyper-pressure and temperature, and hypo- taste and odor. The abnormal perception produces what is termed sensory agnosia, or an inability to attach meaning to sensory impressions. Much of the input coming to these children appears to create antagonism between input, with the child's ultimate interpretation being determined by the interplay between the various dysfunctional sensory channels. . . .

Assessment of the Individual

Although there are some patterns being identified in "autistic" children, general assumptions should not be made about individuals. Each child must be observed as the unique individual he or she is. Knowledge of children with similar problems, however, can provide insights that can greatly assist in the diagnostic and therapeutic processes.

Treatment

Treatment of the child with a sensory dysfunction is multifaceted, including components of neurological organization, specific sensory training, design of a protected sensory environment, behavior management, as well as general medical and nutritional care. The sensory environment is of utmost importance to these children.

Coupling these problems of hyper, hypo, and agitated responses with antagonism between incoming sensory input produces the vital need for a controlled sensory environment. Many "autistic" children, when placed in a controlled environment, respond immediately to the new non-threatening environment. . . .

Rapid, clean (free of extraneous stimuli) presentation has been the key. The same key we have discovered that turns on the "normal" preschool child; the same key that enables many other children who supposedly couldn't learn, to learn. We have ascertained things about perception and sensory function from our "autistic" children that are helping us understand more about the entire learning process.

It is unfortunate that we live in an age of specialization, rigidity, and segregation when there is so much we can learn from each other. As our insights become clearer, hopefully more doors will open, and we can help more of these children come closer to achieving their full potentials.

Portions of this article reprinted with permission of the Journal of the National Academy of Child Development

To see the entire article, Visit NACD's Web site at www.nacd.org.

Resources

For parenting, Christian living, and theology:

- GROWING FAMILIES INTERNATIONAL, INC.
  Address: 3910 Royal Ave. Unit B, Simi Valley, CA 93063
  Phone: (800) 474-6264
  Web address: www.gfi.org

- GRACE AND TRUTH BOOKS
  Address: 3406 Summit Boulevard, Sand Springs, OK 74063
  Phone: (918) 245-1500
  E-mail: 76522.1451@compuserve.com
  Web address: www.graceandtruthbooks.com

- TRINITY BOOK SERVICE
  Address: P.O. Box 395, Montville, NJ 07045
  Phone: (800) 722-3584
  Web address: www.TrinityBookService.org

For information on vitamin therapy and to obtain an E2 diagnostic check-list or other information on autism and related disorders:

- THE AUTISM RESEARCH INSTITUTE
  Address: 4182 Adams Avenue, San Diego, CA 92116
  Web address: www.autism.com/ari/

For information, resources, and support in raising your special needs child:

- NATHHAN (NATIONAL CHALLENGED HOMESCHOOLERS ASSOCIATED NETWORK)
  Address: P.O. Box 39, Porthill, ID 83853
  Phone: (208) 267-6246
  E-mail: NATHANEWS@aol.com
  Web address: http://www.NATHHAN.com

For legal information concerning homeschooling your special needs child:
- HSLDA (HOME SCHOOL LEGAL DEFENSE ASSOCIATION)
  Address: P.O. Box 3000, Purcellville, VA 20134
  Phone: (540)338-5600
  Web address: www.hslda.org

For nutrition and health information:
- LIFE BALANCES, INC.
  Address: P.O. Box 28921, Spokane, WA 99228-8921
  Phone: (509) 455-9976
  Web address: http://www.lifebalances.com

For testing and the providing of a home program for your special needs child:
- NACD (NATIONAL ASSOCIATION FOR CHILD DEVELOPMENT)
  Address: P.O. Box 380, Huntsville, Utah 84317-0380
  Phone: (801) 621-8606
  Web address: www.nacd.org

- HELP WITH LEARNING—NEUROEDUCATIONAL CONSULTANTS OF BOSTON
  Virginia H. Brunelle
  Address: 28 Rockingham St., Lynn, MA 01902
  Phone/fax: (781) 593-1329
  E-mail: RIPSKIPPY@aol.com
  Cities served: All of New England. Most evaluations conducted in Revere, MA.

- CHILD DEVELOPMENT CLINIC
  Craig Stellpflug, BCT, Child Neurodevelopment Consultant
  Clinic Director
  Address: 1009 Hospital Drive Suite 4, Tyler, TX 75701
  Phone: (903) 533-8788
  E-mail: CraigStell@aol.com
  Web address: www.candofoundation.org
  Serving the south central USA

International Christian Association of NeuroDevelopmentalists (ICAN)

ICAN is an international organization responsible for certification, research, training, and progressing the field of NeuroDevelopment. All members of ICAN make a statement of faith. The following individuals provide an individually designed home program, both therapeutic and educational, for your special needs child.

Web address: www.ICAN-DO.org

- CHRISTIAN ACCESS TO NEURODEVELOPMENTAL ORGANIZATION (CAN-DO)
Cyndi Ringoen B.A., B.S., NeuroDevelopmentalist, ICAN certified
Address: P.O. Box 9822, Spokane, WA 99209
Phone: (509) 292-2937
E-mail: cdarling@icehouse.net
Web addresses: members.xoom.com/_XOOM/neupaths/index.htm
http://members.xoom.com/neupaths/
Branches in Seattle, WA; Spokane, WA; Alaska, Simi Valley, CA; Dayton, OH; South Bend, IN, and Trenton, MI.

- HOPE AND A FUTURE
Linda M. Kane, NeuroDevelopmentalist, ICAN certified
Address: P.O. Box 13646, Ogden, UT 84412-3646
Phone: (801) 395-1979
E-mail: hopeandafuture@hotmail.com
Cities served: Wichita, KS; Annapolis, MD; Boise, ID; Chicago, IL; Seattle, WA; cities throughout Wisconsin

- HOPE CENTRE FOR NEUROEDUCATIONAL DEVELOPMENT
Elizabeth Harms, B.Th, NeuroDevelopmentalist, ICAN certified
Address: Box 64, Quill Lake, SK SOA 3EO Canada
Phone/fax: (306) 383-4113
E-mail: hopecentre@sk.sympatico.ca
Web address: www.geocities.com/Athens/Sparta/9442/
Serving families from all over Canada and north central U.S.

- CREAGANLIOS CHILD DEVELOPMENT
  Thomas R. Simmons, B.S., J.D., C.N.C., C.S.N., A.A.C.C.
  NeuroDevelopmentalist, ICAN certified
  Certified Sports Nutritionist, IFPA
  American Assn. of Christian Counselors
  Address: P.O. Box 60, Westmoreland, NH 03467
  Phone: (603) 357-8031
  Fax: (603) 357-8964
  E-mail: creagchild@monad.net
  Web address: www.creaganlios.com
  Evaluation locations: Plainville, CT; Portland, ME; Waldoboro, ME; Worcester, MA; Manchester, NH; Keene, NH; Albany, NY; Brattleboro, VT

- NEUROEDUCATIONAL CONSULTANTS OF INDIANA
  Marcia Blackwood, M.Ed., NeuroDevelopmentalist, ICAN certified
  Address: 2320 Sloan Avenue, Indianapolis, IN 46203-4850
  Phone: (317) 375-1775
  Fax: (317) 375-1785
  E-mail: marciablackwood@juno.com
  Web address: http://members.tripod.com/~MarciaBlackwood-Indy/
  Serving families in Indiana, Illinois, Kentucky, Ohio, Missouri, and Wisconsin

- HELP WITH LEARNING NEUROEDUCATIONAL CONSULTING
  Marilee Nicoll Coots, B.A., NeuroDevelopmentalist, ICAN certified
  Address: 20651 Hwy 178, Weldon, CA 93283
  Phone: 760-378-4357 or 760-378-4204
  E-mail: helpwithlearning@juno.com
  Web address: http://members.tripod.com/~helpwithlearning/
  Cities served: San Diego, Burbank, Huntington Beach, Bakersfield, Weldon, and Simi Valley, CA

- SOUTHEASTERN NEURODEVELOPMENTAL CONSULTANTS (SENC)
  Kay Ness, M.S., Certified NeuroDevelopmentalist, ICAN certified
  Address: 4920 Hwy 9, Suite 351, Alpharetta, GA 30004
  Phone/fax: 770-619-9843
  E-mail: kness@avana.net
  Web address: www.senc.org
  Serving Georgia, Alabama, Florida, eastern Tennessee, western
  North Carolina, Atlanta, and central Florida.